Learning English

English for Health and Social Care Workers

Ros Wright and Richard Cresswell

ENGLISH TEACHING *professional*

Pavilion

A study guide for speakers of c... nd social care

English for Health and Social Care

Published by:
Pavilion Publishing and Media Ltd
Rayford House
School Road
Hove BN3 5HX
UK

Tel: 01273 434 943
Fax: 01273 227 308

First published 2017

A catalogue record for this book is available from the British Library.

ISBN: 978-1-911028-07-9

Pavilion is the leading publisher and provider of professional development products and services for workers in the health, social care, education and community safety sectors. We believe that everyone has the right to fulfill their potential and we strive to supply products and services that help raise standards, promote best practices and support continuing professional development.

Authors: Ros Wright and Richard Cresswell

Development editor: Helena Gomm

Production editor: Mike Benge, Pavilion Publishing and Media

Cover design: Phil Morash, Pavilion Publishing and Media

Page layout and typesetting: Phil Morash, Pavilion Publishing and Media

Printing: Newman Thomson

Contents

To play the audio tracks and to find the audio transcripts and exercise answers, go to:
www.etprofessional.com/english-for-health-social-care

Foreword

by Des Kelly OBE, Executive Director, National Care Forum

Effective communication is at the very heart of social care. It is difficult to imagine that it would be possible to offer good quality care without it. Communication is a fundamental aspect of relationship-building which, in turn, is necessary to ensure care and support services are appropriately personalised to each individual. Definitions of the best care and support in both health and care settings are typically described in the language of 'personalised' services. In other words, tailored to meet the needs of the individual receiving care and support, and characterised by relationships that respect the rights and dignity of people, promote choice and control, and protect them from abuse or neglect.

The premise of this book is a simple one: those care workers for whom English is not their first language will have particular learning needs to work in health and social care. It is helpful, therefore, that the book adopts a practical approach to the role of providing care and support, starting with the vital importance of effective communication to building relationships. The structured approach taken in the book to the new standards of care within the Care Certificate offers an excellent way to guide study and makes this a very timely publication.

The scope of the book is undoubtedly ambitious – and rightly so. There is a systematic approach to the wide-ranging subject matter, with each aspect of the care task introduced in a practical way incorporating vocabulary, grammar and report writing. The self-study format offers guidance for further reading and study, as well as a checklist for learners. The layout of the material nicely reinforces this reflective style.

Writing in 2017, it would be an oversight not to reference the wider social context within which health and care services are presently operating. Efforts by successive governments to seek to control public-sector funding have resulted in significant pressures, cost reductions and cuts to frontline services. Recruitment and retention remains a significant workforce challenge, especially for nursing staff. There are major regional variations around recruitment and commissioning. Against this backdrop, demographic trends are such that demand for health and care services continues to rise, along with the consumer expectations of the public.

The health and care sectors in England (as elsewhere) are experiencing a period of considerable change and transformation as the legislation of the Care Act (2014) is implemented and as services respond to these wider issues of context. For many health and care service providers, one of the most pressing challenges is that of workforce recruitment and retention. Attracting the right people with the right values and attitudes is essential. Developing and supporting them to ensure that they are appropriately skilled is also vital to creating the necessary conditions for the best quality of personalised care and support to prevail. Ongoing learning and professional development is a crucial aspect of demonstrating to care staff that they are valued and how much their contribution matters to the quality of life for people who receive care and support.

People will be attracted to working in the health and care sectors from a wide variety of backgrounds and experiences. There can be little doubt that this will continue to include people who do not have English as their first language and are new to working in the English health and care sectors. New entrants to health and care have much to learn, and it can seem a hugely daunting task to absorb the knowledge necessary to gain confidence in the role. With the additional need to master the skills of a new language, a structured and systematic method is, therefore, essential in my view. This book does just that. It fills a gap that results from the need to ensure sufficient staff of the right calibre are available to deliver good quality care and that the right skill mix is achieved. The structured and practical format should prove beneficial to new learners as well as more experienced care workers wishing to refresh their knowledge and language skills.

I commend the authors for having the vision to bring together all the learning materials and resources in such a practical way to enable non-English-speaking care workers to prepare for completion of the Care Certificate.

Introduction

The reason for this book is simple – to provide you with a learning resource if you work or are planning to work in social care in frontline services in mental health, learning disability and older people. It addresses many of the topics covered in the *Skills for Care – Care Certificate*, which must be covered by all workers during their induction period in the UK whether they are new to the job or are changing organisations to another job. The course will help you to gain study skills around the many aspects of social care and to develop your English language skills.

English for Health and Social Care Workers covers a number of topics including: safeguarding; health and safety; equality and diversity; report writing; moving and handling; assisting people to eat and drink; supporting people who are distressed; having difficult conversations; negotiating different dialects and accents; dealing with behaviour that challenges; and dealing with medication. Using the book as a study guide, you will be taken through each chapter by the use of various case studies and scenarios that will test your understanding of various situations that you will meet in the course of your working day. These will be everyday situations such as assisting people to make decisions about what they wish to eat or how they want to wash, but also more serious issues such as dealing with potential physical and sexual abuse, behaviour that challenges or dangerous occurrences that may take place in the care setting. The course offers practical guidance on how to deal with situations that may arise and the potential consequences of not following important legislation and organisational policies and procedures.

Another important area that the book looks at is how you communicate with the people that you work with, not just service users but your colleagues and management teams. It provides scenarios that will test your understanding of how to communicate sensitively and effectively in difficult situations, such as when people are distressed or upset or have higher-level communication needs. *English for Health and Social Care Workers* seeks to challenge the way you interact with people and sees communication as a tool that must demonstrate understanding, trust and respect to everyone that you work with. The Core Values run throughout every unit, scenario and case study in the course.

Each text within the book will provide you with the chance to put the Core Values into action and look at why the people you work with must be at the centre of everything you do, and why all decisions that you make must be in the best interests of the service user.

Most of all, this book seeks to start a conversation that will help you to not only improve your English, but to understand why people communicate and the unique and individual needs that each person who enters the care system possesses.

Approach

English for Health and Social Care Workers uses an approach that encourages you to discover the language for yourself, helping you develop language skills that you will need in your place of work on a daily basis, be that in a care home, a hospital or in domiciliary care situations.

Professional texts

Professional texts, e.g. case studies and *Daily Care Reports*, as well as dialogues with service users and colleagues, are used to introduce language and show examples of effective spoken and written communication.

Professional tasks

Tasks you might already carry out in the workplace, such as completing an *ABC Chart* or assisting a service user with their personal care, are replicated throughout the book, depending on the topic of the unit. These tasks will draw on your professional experiences as a carer and help you develop English skills in real-life professional contexts. Role-plays then offer the chance to consolidate this new language and put the skills you have learnt into practice.

Grammar and vocabulary

The book focuses on the grammar structures and vocabulary (including some technical terms) that you will need in order to carry out your responsibilities as a carer and therefore communicate more effectively with service users, their families and your colleagues.

Pronunciation and intonation

The book provides opportunities to improve your pronunciation, for example of key technical and medical terms. You will also learn *how* to use your voice (intonation) to put service users at ease and reassure them. This is essential in developing rapport with service users (and colleagues) and avoiding potential misunderstandings.

Cultural awareness

It is important to understand the culture of your service users (e.g. if they prefer you to use their first name or their family name) as well as the professional culture of your workplace in the UK. The book will encourage you to think about cultural differences and help you develop a positive relationship with your colleagues, your service users and their families.

Written skills

Written skills are equally important to carers working in the UK. Throughout the book there are lots of opportunities to practise filling in charts and writing basic reports, which will train you to write clearly, coherently and with accuracy.

Special features

In their shoes

Many of the units begin with a series of activities that introduces the topic, such as Personal Care (Unit 2), and encourages you to think about it from the point of view of the service user, eg *'How would you feel if another person had to help you with your personal care (going to the toilet, taking a shower, etc.)?'* This reflective activity will help you better understand, and therefore build rapport with, your service users.

Case studies

Throughout the book you will meet several service users, known as 'case studies'. You will learn about the relevant personal details of these service users as well as information you might need in order to provide their care. Case studies include Martin, who has muscular dystrophy and requires constant 24-hour care, and Irene, an 87-year-old widow living independently but with decreased mobility.

Medical focus

As you go through the book you will learn about health-related subjects and conditions that are typically experienced by service users in the UK. These include names for parts of the body, type 2 diabetes, pressure sores, strokes and autism, among others. You will learn the specific medical terms related to these conditions as well as how to assist service users when necessary.

Audio tracks

Throughout the book you will be directed to listen to recorded conversations between various carers and service users, as well as colleagues and family members. When you see an audio track number at the start of a question, go to www.etprofessional.com/english-for-health-social-care and listen to the corresponding track eg

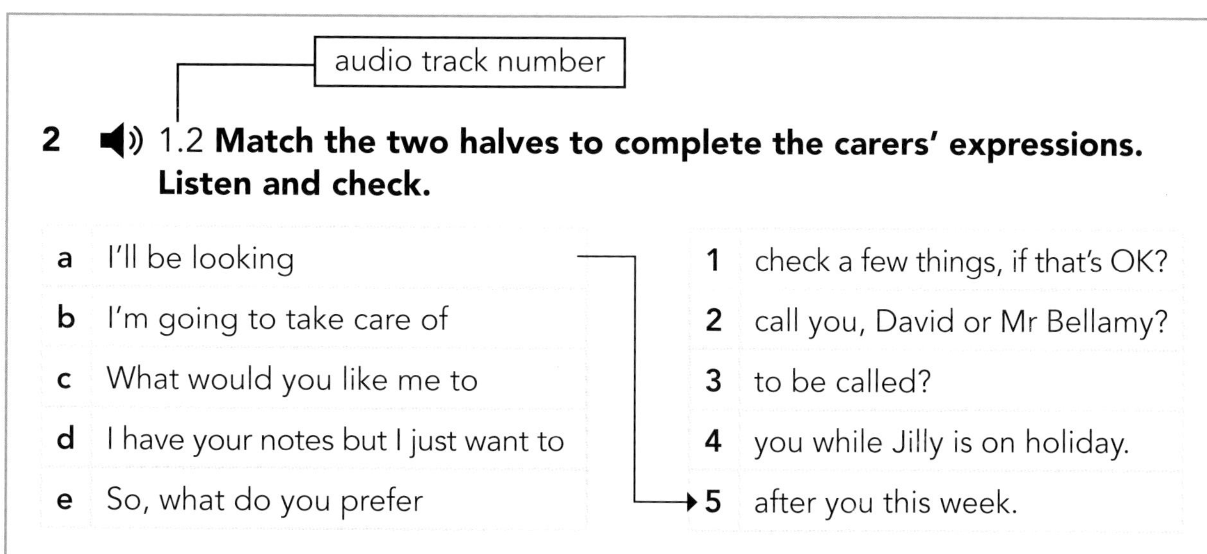

2 1.2 **Match the two halves to complete the carers' expressions. Listen and check.**

a	I'll be looking	1	check a few things, if that's OK?
b	I'm going to take care of	2	call you, David or Mr Bellamy?
c	What would you like me to	3	to be called?
d	I have your notes but I just want to	4	you while Jilly is on holiday.
e	So, what do you prefer	5	after you this week.

After listening to each audio track you will be asked a number of questions about it to test your understanding and your ability to extract information from a spoken text. The transcripts for these conversations are online (www.etprofessional.com/english-for-health-social-care).

Answers

Also available online (www.etprofessional.com/english-for-health-social-care) are the answers to all of the questions in this book. You can use these to check your responses to the questions once you have completed a task.

We hope you enjoy using *English for Health and Social Care Workers* and that you achieve success in your career as a social care worker in the UK or elsewhere.

Ros Wright and Richard Cresswell

To play the audio tracks and to find the audio transcripts and exercise answers, go to:
www.etprofessional.com/english-for-health-social-care

Unit 1

Communication

Target areas

- Working in social care • Introducing yourself and establishing rapport
- Effective communication in social care • Asking questions
- Making social conversation • Medical focus: body parts

Working in social care

1 The pictures below show some of the responsibilities of social carers. Label them with the terms in the box.

managing finances and budgeting	~~ordering and collecting prescriptions~~
preparing meals	administering medication
assisting with travel	delivering personal care
helping with shopping	carrying out cleaning duties

a *ordering and collecting prescriptions*

b

c

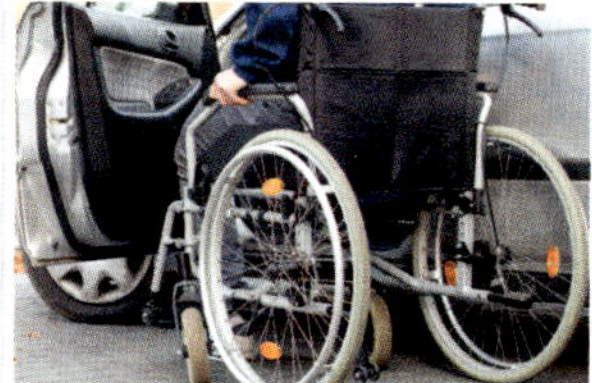

d

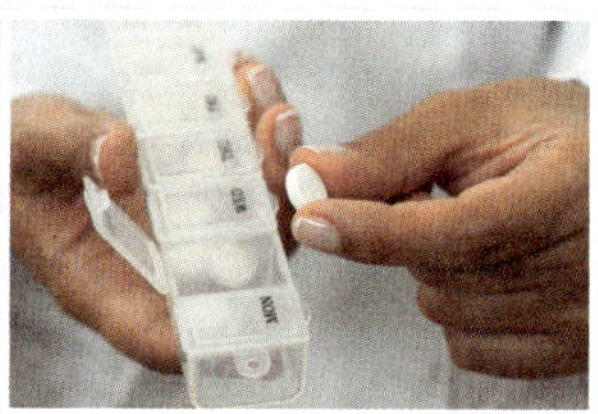

e

f

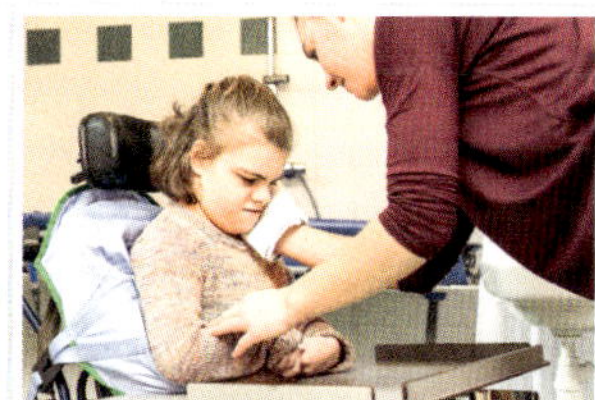

g

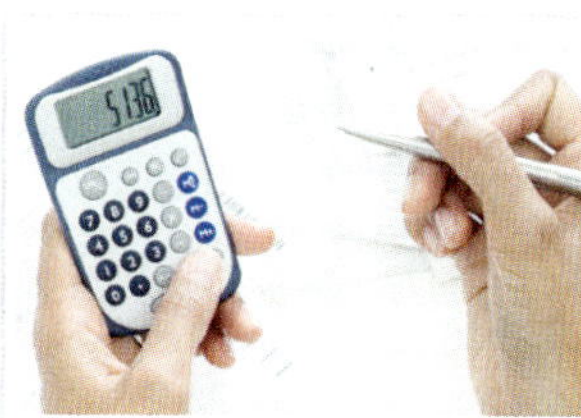

h

2 Write down two or three other tasks that carers carry out.

eg *writing reports about service users*

3 1.1 **Listen as three carers describe their job. Circle the correct letter(s) of the responsibilities discussed in 1 (p11).**

a	Polly	a	b	c	d	e	f	(g)	h
b	Steve	a	b	c	d	e	f	g	h
c	Maryssa	a	b	c	d	e	f	g	h

4 1.1 **Listen again and complete the table below.**

	likes	dislikes
Polly		
Steve		
Maryssa		

Introducing yourself and establishing rapport

1 1.2 **Listen and complete the expressions Steve and Maryssa use to introduce themselves.**

a Good morning, __________ today? __________ Steve...

b Hello, it's Mrs Driver, __________? I'm Maryssa. __________ last year.

2 1.2 **Match the two halves to complete the carers' expressions. Listen and check.**

a	I'll be looking → 5	1	check a few things, if that's OK?
b	I'm going to take care of	2	call you, David or Mr Bellamy?
c	What would you like me to	3	to be called?
d	I have your notes but I just want to	4	you while Jilly is on holiday.
e	So, what do you prefer	5	after you this week.

3 It's important to use the person's preferred name. Add vowels (a, e, i, o, u) to complete the service users' expressions.

a J_st c_ll m_ Delia.

b Y_u c_n c_ll m_ Jim.

c My n_m_'s Nancy, b_t m_st pe_pl_ c_ll m_ Nan.

d I pr_f_r t_ b_ c_ll_d by my s_rn_me.

4 1.3 **Listen to the questions being asked and pay attention to how the carer's voices go up and down as they speak. We do this to sound more friendly.**

a Good morning, how are you today?

b Hello, it's Mrs Driver, isn't it?

c What would you like me to call you, David or Mr Bellamy?

d I have your notes, but I just want to check a few things, if that's OK?

e What do you prefer to be called?

5 1.3 **Now listen and repeat what you hear. Your voice should go up and down as you speak.**

Effective communication in social care

1 Read the following quotation. Do you agree? Why (not)?

'Communication is an essential part of a caring relationship and helps to encourage trusting relationships with the individuals you care for.'

(The Care Certificate Workbook, Standard 6, www.skillsforcare.org.uk)

2 Read the text about communication below and answer the questions that follow.

Communication, Part 1

Effective (good) communication is essential to establish and maintain a positive relationship between carers and their service users. It helps carers to understand the individual and provide better care. Communication is a two-way process. The speaker delivers a message, and the listener shows they understand the message through their verbal and non-verbal language ie facial expression (smiling) or gesture (nodding or shaking the head). However, there are many things that stop the communication process ('barriers to communication'), which can cause confusion, even distress, for the service user.

a How does good communication help the carer?

b Give two examples of non-verbal communication.

c What do we mean by 'barriers to communication'?

3 Write down five barriers to communication. Use the following pictures to help you.

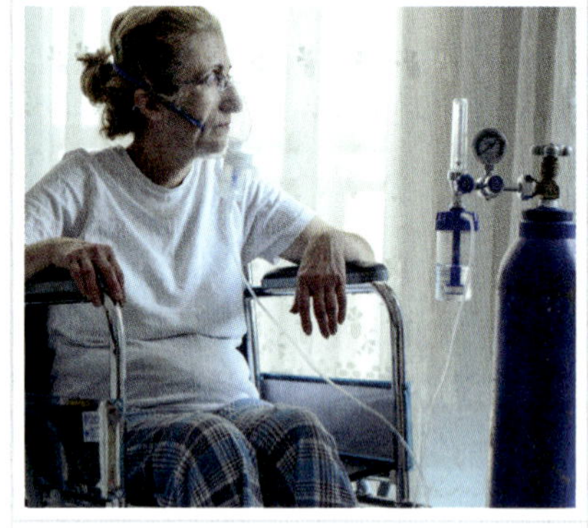
a

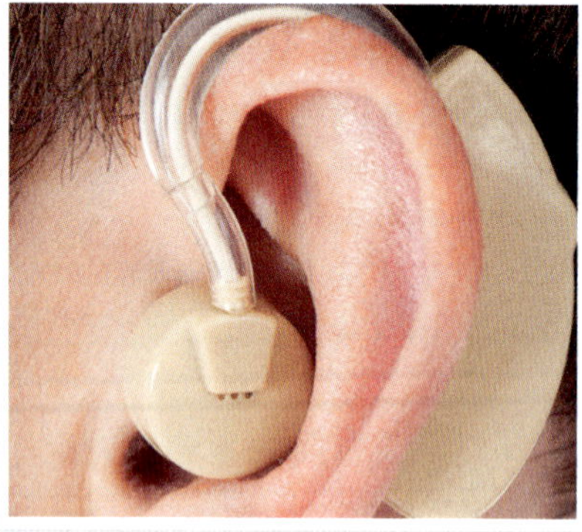
b

c

d e

4 Read the text below and check your answers to 3. Underline more barriers to communication.

Communication, Part 2

Common barriers to communication might include background noise, accents and dialects. Sensory impairment, such as deafness, can make communication difficult, as can certain physical conditions eg breathlessness or being in pain, and negative emotions or feelings. Both negative body language eg crossed arms, giving the impression of anger, and personal space (position between people) are also major barriers to communication. A person who sits too far away may show a lack of interest in the speaker, while sitting too close can be intimidating.

5 Think about service users from different cultures. What other barriers to communication are there?

6 Go online and find out about these other forms of communication used with service users:

- Braille
- British Sign Language (BSL)
- Makaton

7 1.4 **Service users speak in a variety of accents and dialects. Listen and add vowels (*a, e, i, o u*) to complete these local greetings.**

a Y_m _lright chick? **West Midlands**

b Ay _p me d_ck. **East Midlands/South Yorkshire**

c W_tch_ darlin'. **London**

d Why _y_ pet? **Newcastle (Geordie)**

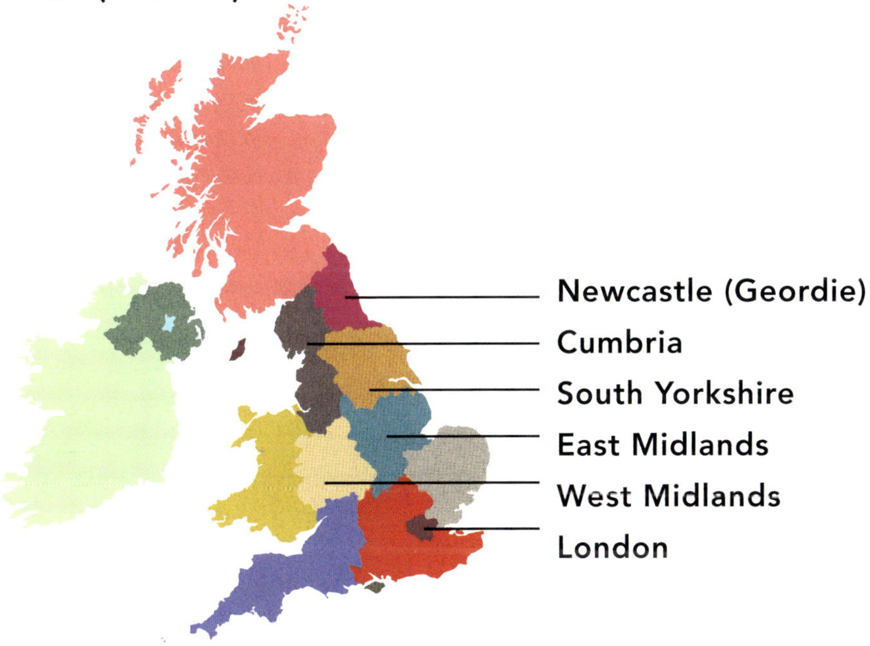

Newcastle (Geordie)
Cumbria
South Yorkshire
East Midlands
West Midlands
London

8 Would you use terms of endearment (duck, chick, pet) with service users? Why (not)?

9 Read about service user Joe Boden.

Joe Boden (90) has lived for most of his life in Newcastle in the north of England. He is fairly independent and lives in his own home. Joe is alert and lively and enjoys the daily interaction with his carers.

10 🔊 1.5 **Listen to Joe talking to his new carer, Miro from Bulgaria. Why is communication difficult between Miro and Joe?**

11 🔊 1.5 **Listen again and complete Miro's expressions.**

Miro: Good morning, Joe, I'm Miro. It's **(a)** ____________.

Joe: Alreet, boy, lad.

Miro: Sorry, sir, **(b)** ____________.

Joe: Hello, come on away!

Miro: **(c)** ____________ you want me to leave?

Joe: No, lad. It means come in, like!

Miro: Oh yes, thank you.

Joe: It's gay cold out there, eh?

Miro: Sorry, Joe, can **(d)** ____________?

Joe: I said it's 'gay cold out there' – it means it's very cold, like.

Miro: Oh, OK. You're right, it's very cold today.

12 Think about elderly service users you know and answer these questions.

a How do your service users react when they don't understand you?

b What do you do to help them understand you?

13 Choose one expression from each box (1–4) to form statements to facilitate communication.

1	2	3	4
I'm from Bulgaria. You've probably noticed I'm not from round here. Maybe you can hear I have an accent.	(so) I may (so) I apologise if I	ask you to repeat things from time to time. have to ask you to repeat something.	Sorry about that. I'm sorry. Apologies.

eg *I'm from Bulgaria, so I may ask you to repeat things from time to time. Sorry about that.*

14 Re-order these words to form expressions to reassure your service user.

a Please / don't understand / you / stop me / if

b Let me / repeat anything / you need / know if / me to

Grammar focus: Asking questions

1 Read about using WH words to ask questions.

Use WH words – **what, where, who, why, when** and **how** – to ask questions.	***What*** time is it? ***How*** do you feel today?

2 Use WH words to complete these carers' questions.

a <u>*What*</u> do you want for breakfast?

b _____ is your GP?

c _____ is the bathroom?

d _____ will your daughter visit you next?

e _____ is the heating on? It's July.

f _____ old are you?

3 Use WH words and write five more questions you frequently ask service users.

4 <u>Underline</u> the correct words in *italics* to complete the definitions.

a *Closed / Open* questions need a *Yes/No* or simple one-word answer.

b *Closed / Open* questions encourage service users to give detailed answers.

c *Closed / Open* questions ask service users to give brief, factual information.

d *Closed / Open* questions use verbs like *tell, explain* and *describe.*

e *Closed / Open* questions encourage conversation.

5 Which question in 2 is an open question? Why?

6 Look at these questions and tick (✓) 'Open' or 'Closed' for each one.

		Open	**Closed**
a	How can I help you today?	✓	
b	What's a typical day like for you?		
c	Do you usually have toast or cereal for breakfast?		
d	Are you OK?		
e	What was your husband like?		
f	Where does your son live now?		
g	Did you go out shopping today?		
h	What kinds of programmes do you like to watch on TV?		

7 Now match the answers below to the correct question in 6.

1	Not really.	d	5	Toast.	
2	He was a lovely gentle man and he loved spending time with his kids. I really miss him.		6	Could you help me do the cleaning?	
3	He's in Glasgow.		7	No, I didn't.	
4	I prefer crime and hospital dramas, but I also like watching the news.		8	I get up at seven and have breakfast. Then I go to the day centre for a few hours. I eat lunch ...	

8 Rewrite these closed questions as open questions.

a Are you OK?

b Where does your son live now?

c Did you go out shopping today?

d Do you usually have toast or cereal for breakfast?

9 🔊 1.6 **Listen and repeat what you hear. Notice how the speaker's voice goes up and down in a friendly way as he/she speaks. Practise the open questions from 6 and 8 in the same way.**

10 Read about service user June Talbot. Which of the responsibilities on p11 do you think carers Polly and Yemi will need to carry out?

June Talbot (78) lives in her own home with her daughter, Cheryl (52). June recently had a stroke, leaving her with slurred speech and unable to weight bear (stand without assistance). She now requires the support of two carers for an hour, three times a day.

11 🔊 1.7 **Listen to a conversation with June and Cheryl and check your answers to 10.**

12 🔊 1.7 **Listen to Part 1 and <u>underline</u> the words in *italics* to complete the statements.**

a June has *<u>met Polly</u> / never met Polly or Yemi / met Yemi* before.

b In the mornings, Polly and Yemi will help June to *get dressed / wash and dress / have a bath*.

c June is *hearing impaired / sight impaired / physically disabled*.

13 🔊 1.7 **Listen to Part 2 and write down June's typical daily food intake.**

Include: breakfast, lunch, evening meal

14 🔊 1.7 **Listen to Part 3 and <u>underline</u> the words in *italics* to complete the statements.**

a The carers will *telephone / ring the doorbell / knock* and wait before entering the house.

b The previous carers were *very noisy / disrespectful / lazy*.

c June and Cheryl should inform the carers if they are *unhappy / happy* with the carers' service.

15 Look at this part of the dialogue. Why does the communication process fail?

Polly: Excellent! Now, how do you like to wash, June? Morning or night or both? Do you prefer a bath or a shower?

June: Sorry, what did you say, dear?

16 🔊 1.7 **Polly asks new questions. Add WH words to complete her questions. Listen to Part 1 and check.**

a **Polly:** _____ do you like to wash?

June: I like a shower in the morning.

b **Polly:** And _____ about the evening?

June: Oh, I just like to freshen up with a flannel usually.

17 🔊 1.7 **Complete the carers' questions. Listen to Part 2 and answer the questions.**

	Question	Answer
a	So tell us, ______________ food do you like for breakfast?	Toast and ______________
b	______________ lunch?	
c	And ______________ your evening meals, June?	
d	And ______________?	

18 Practise asking the questions in 16 and 17. Make sure your voice sounds friendly.

Making social conversation

1 🔊 1.8 **Listen to a carer talking to service user Phyllis. What is their main topic of conversation?**

2 🔊 1.8 **Listen again and complete the carer's questions.**

a ____________ your family.

b ____________ they?

c ____________ locally?

d ____________ the rest of the family?

3 Label the topics of conversation for older service users with the words in the box. Then write two or three more possible topics.

~~family~~	food	TV programmes	weather	news and current affairs

a *family*

b

c

d

e

4 Write down three or four possible topics of conversation for younger service users.

eg *music*

5 Match the two halves to complete the following questions. More than one answer may be possible.

a	What do you enjoy	1	the new Prime Minister?
b	Do you like	2	what happened in Cumbria yesterday?
c	Tell me about	3	doing?
d	Anything interesting	4	your birthday?
e	What do you think about	5	on the TV last night?
f	Did you read about	6	the book you're reading.
g	What did you do for	7	playing cards?

(a → 3)

6 Use the question beginnings from 5 (a–g) to write new questions, using the prompts below.

eg *Do you like watching sport? / Tell me about your favourite sport.*

a sport **b** article / royal baby **c** the papers / today
d friends and family **e** dance **f** grandchildren
g Christmas

7 There are different ways to encourage conversation. Categorise each of the expressions in the boxes into one of the columns below.

~~Really?~~	Oh no!	You're joking.	~~That's terrible.~~	Uh-huh.
That's great.	Wow!	That's interesting.	I'm really pleased (for you).	
Excellent.	What a shame.	That's wonderful.	How awful.	Mmmm.
How exciting.	1972!			

Show interest	Show positive agreement	Show negative agreement
Really?		*That's terrible.*

8 Add the expressions from 7 to these mini dialogues. More than one answer is possible.

a	My grandchildren are going to Disneyland Paris next week.	
b	My neighbour was in a car crash yesterday.	
c	I played the lottery last week, but I didn't win anything.	
d	My best friend is coming over from Australia soon. I haven't seen her since 1972.	

9 Look at the transcript for 1.8 online. Find the language the carer uses to encourage conversation with Phyllis.

10 1.9 **Listen to the dialogues and repeat what you hear. Take the role of the carer.**

Medical focus: Parts of the body

1 Label the body parts with the terms in the boxes.

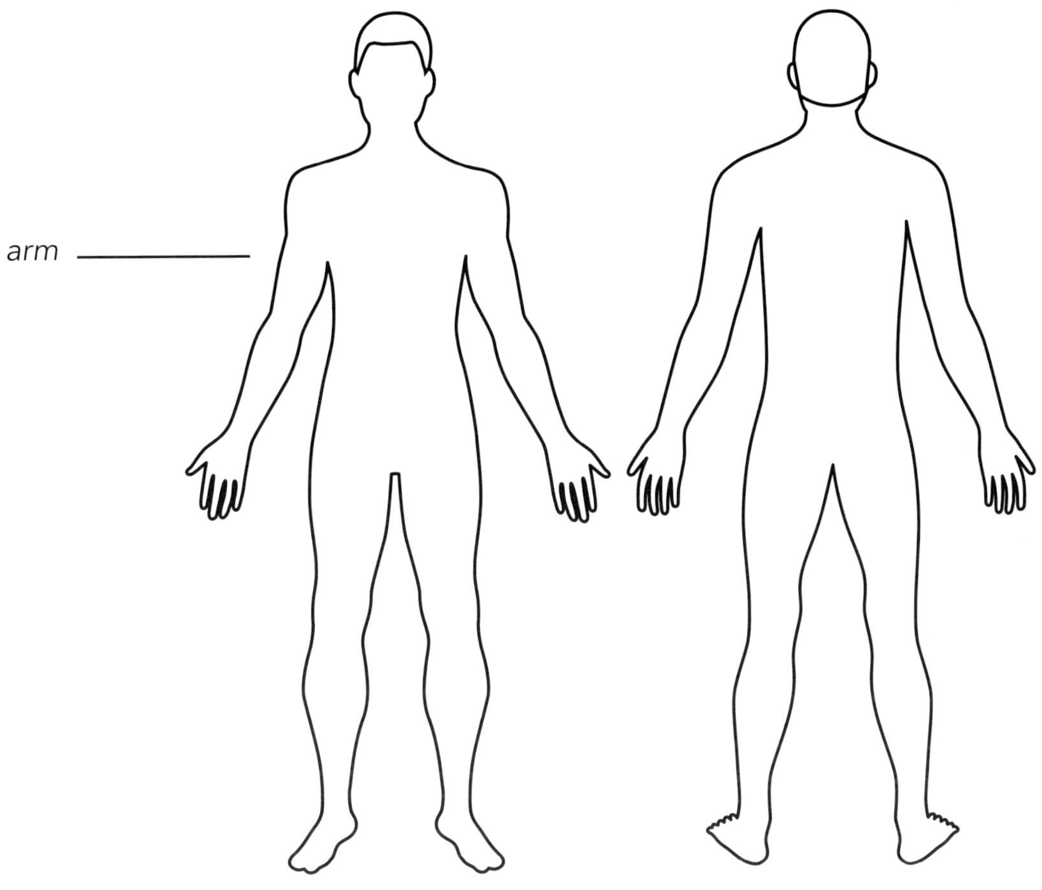

~~arm~~	back	thumb	buttocks	face	finger	foot	groin	hand
leg	neck	shoulder	head	hip	stomach	toe	breast/chest	

2 Label the head and face with the words in the boxes.

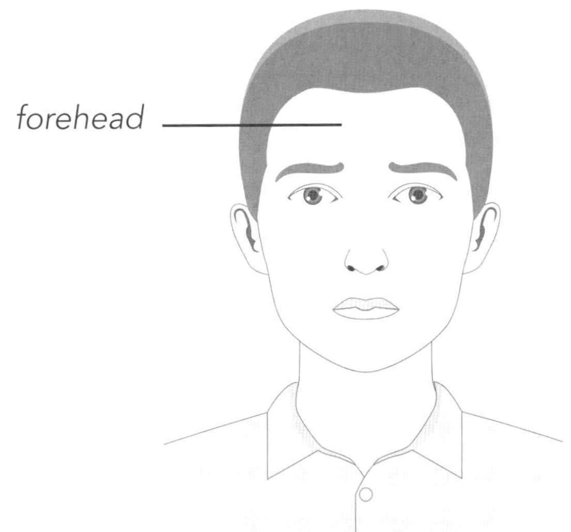

~~forehead~~	lips	chin	cheek	cheekbone	eyelash	ear	nose
eyebrow	neck	crown	eye	nostril	jaw	collar bone	

3 Put each of these terms into the correct category.

~~ankle~~	~~arm~~	armpit	calf	elbow	finger	foot	hand
knee	leg	shin	thigh	thumb	toe	wrist	

Upper limb (arm)	Lower limb (leg)
arm	*ankle*

4 Underline the word(s) that don't belong.

a **Trunk (body):** groin, neck, *face*, shoulder

b **Face:** eyelid, shin, cheekbone, wrist

c **Upper limb:** arm, armpit, buttock, calf, elbow, finger, hand, hip, thumb

d **Head:** nostril, collarbone, ear, crown

e **Lower limb:** ankle, armpit, foot, knee, leg, shin, thigh, toe, wrist

Unit 2

Personal care

Target areas

• Assisting with personal hygiene and grooming • Future review (*will* versus *going to*)
• Talking about bodily functions • Assisting with toileting • Medical focus: UTIs
• Offering help • Report writing (1)

In their shoes

1 It's important to understand what it's like to be a service user. Write four or five adjectives about how would you feel if you were dependent on others for your personal care?

eg *humiliated*

2 Read the following quotation. What does *'cater to their individual habits and preferences'* mean?

'Being dependent on others for washing, bathing and using the toilet is humiliating for most people, therefore it is important to protect the patient's dignity and to try to cater for their individual habits and preferences.'

(*Culture, Religion and Patient Care in a Multi-ethnic Society: A handbook for professionals by Alix Henley and Judith Schott, Age Concern Books, 1999*)

Assisting with personal hygiene and grooming

1 Put the items used for personal care into the correct category. Use a dictionary if necessary.

Washing	Dental care	Grooming
soap		*deodorant*

2 🔊 2.1 **Listen and tick (✓) the correct box to complete the personal care chart for each service user.**

Personal care	Doreen	Ted	Howard
Complete bed bath			
Partial bed bath			
Bath/shower			
Skin care: lotion/massage			

Personal care	Doreen	Ted	Howard
Oral care/denture care			
Shave			
Shampoo/hair care			
Foot care: lotion/soak			
Nail care			
Remove/apply elastic hose			
Dress or assist			
Weigh			

3 2.1 **Listen again. Which personal care items do the carers use?**

a Doreen *toothbrush* ______________

b Ted ______________

c Howard ______________ ______________

4 Read the information about service user Irene Matthews. What does her carer, Polly, need to think about when assisting with her personal care?

eg *Irene's ability to move (her mobility)*

Irene Matthews (87) lived with her husband until he died 10 years ago. Since then her mobility has decreased. She is unable to walk far unaided and moved into sheltered accommodation two years ago. Her daughter Megan (58) lives close by, visits most days and works in close partnership with her mother and the carers. Irene's son, Tony, lives in London but has little contact. Irene is very sociable and enjoys her visits from the carers and her daughter, as well as attending the day centre twice a week.

5 🔊 2.2 **Listen to Part 1. <u>Underline</u> the correct words in *italics* to complete the statements below.**

a Ms Matthews wants to *have a bath / wash at the sink / have a shower.*

b Ms Matthews is wearing *a nightdress / pyjamas / a dress.*

c Ms Matthews is *not able / is able* to get into the bath without assistance from her carer.

d Ms Matthews uses a bath-board and a *bath chair /non-slip mat* to steady her in the shower.

6 Look at these stages for washing a service user. Number them in the correct order (1–8).

a	Assist service user to undress.		
b	Wash or assist service user to wash themselves.		
c	Assist service user into the shower or bath.		
d	Place bath-board, shower chair etc. into bath or shower/sink area.		
e	Assist service user to the bathroom.		
f	Ask service user their preference – bath, shower or wash at the sink.	*1*	
g	Put on Personal Protective Equipment (PPE).		
h	Check temperature of water.		

7 🔊 2.2 **Listen to Part 1 again. Tick (✓) the stages in 6 that Polly carries out.**

8 🔊 2.2 **Match two halves to complete Polly's expressions. Listen and check. Practise saying the expressions aloud.**

a	Are you ready	→ 4	1	if you need to.
b	Let's get		2	get undressed?
c	Can I help you		3	temperature of the water.
d	Let me just check the		4	for your morning wash?
e	Hold on to me		5	your walking frame.

9 🔊 2.2 **Listen to Part 2 and complete Polly's expressions.**

a How's the water? <u>*OK for you?*</u>

b Let me know when you're ______________________________.

c Let me just put a ____.

d Would you like to ______________________________________?

10 🔊 2.3 **Listen and repeat Polly's questions.**
Make sure you follow the intonation pattern you hear. What happens to the intonation patterns in c?

a Are you ready for your morning wash?

b Can I help you get undressed?

c How's the water for you?

d Would you like to brush your teeth?

11 Use the prompts in the boxes and practise these expressions. Use the correct intonation pattern.

wash hair/back/feet	do hair/back/teeth	brush teeth/hair	clean fingernails/toenails

Let me know when you're ready to ...

(Your voice should go down when you use this structure.)

Would you like to ...

(Your voice should go up when you use this structure.)

Grammar focus: *will* versus *going to*

1 Read about how we use *going to* and *will* to talk about the future.

Use ***going to*** + infinitive to inform the service user about proposed actions and to talk about planned events.	We use ***will*** + infinitive for decisions we make at the moment of speaking or predictions.
▶ I'm ***going to help*** you get dressed. (action)	▶ I'***ll help*** you put your coat on. (decision)
▶ Are you ***going to see*** your son today? (planned event)	▶ You'***ll feel*** better tomorrow. (prediction)

2 **Look at transcripts** 2.1 **and** 2.2 **online and find examples of *going to* and *will*.**

eg *I'm just going to put the bath-board in the bath. I'll give you a hand.*

3 🔊 2.4 **Complete these expressions with either *I'm going to* or *I will (I'll)*. Then listen and check.**

a _____________ wash my hands first and put on my apron.

b _________ just wait outside the door. Tell me when you're ready.

c I think you've got a temperature, __________ call the doctor.

d What time __________ you __________ visit your daughter?

e __________ check the temperature of the water.

REMEMBER!

Always check with your service user before you do something. This is called 'asking for consent'. Here's how to ask for consent:

- I'm going to … . Is that OK/alright (with you)?
- I'm going to … if that's alright/OK (with you).

Practise asking for consent aloud.

eg I'm going to start with your back. Is that OK?
I'm going to start with your back, if that's alright with you.

Assisting with dressing

1 Write the correct verbs for dressing under each picture.

~~do up~~	loosen	pull down	pull up	put on
roll up	roll down	take off	tighten	~~undo~~

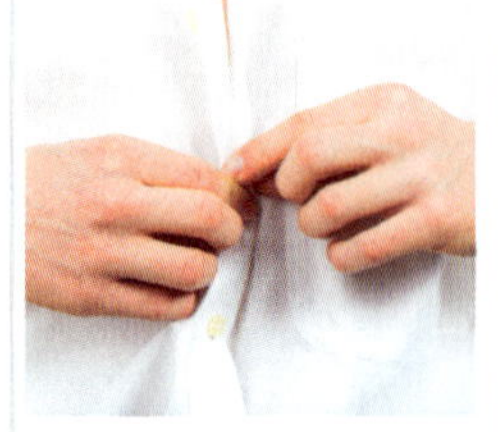		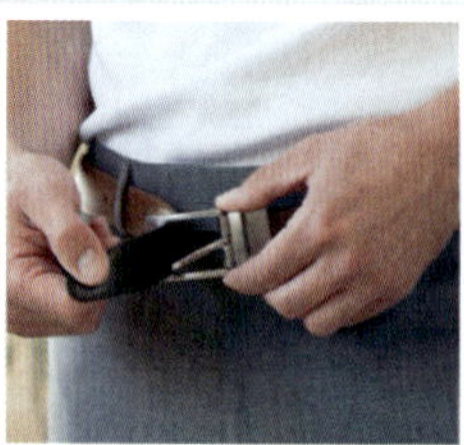	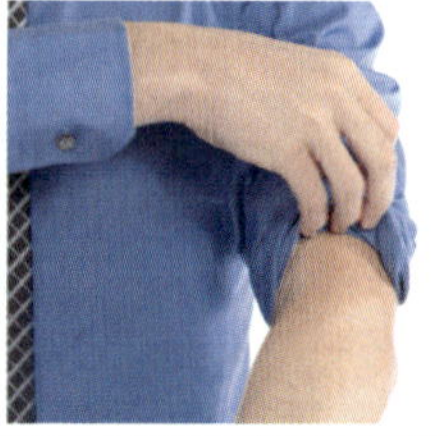	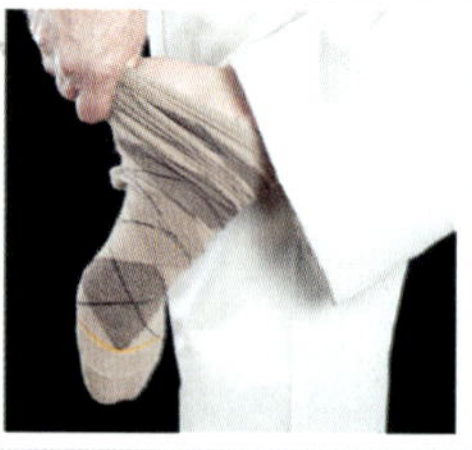
a *undo / do up*	b ____ / _____	c ____ / _____	d ____ / _____	e ____ / _____

2 Now choose the best verb(s) for each group of items.

a clothes, shoes, make-up, jewellery — pull up / roll down / <u>*take off*</u> / tighten / undo

b jeans, zip, trousers, buttons, skirt — pull up / roll down / take off / tighten / undo

c	socks, tights, sleeve	pull up / roll down / take off / tighten / undo
d	trousers, belt, jeans	pull up / roll down / take off / tighten / undo
e	trousers, shirt, skirt, pants	pull up / roll down / take off / tighten / undo

3 These dressing aids can help service users to maintain their independence. Label the pictures with the words in the boxes.

dressing stick	shoe horn	sock aid	stocking aid
a __________	b __________	c __________	d __________

Dressing aid images a, c, d are used with permission from Welcome Mobility. www.welcomemobility.co.uk

4 Write explanations to show how to use the aids in 3. Practise saying them aloud.

eg *Stocking aid: first, put your stocking over the round part. Then ….*

5 2.2 **Listen to Part 3. Write T (true) or F (false) for each statement.**

a	Ms Matthews doesn't use any dressing aids.	*F*
b	Ms Matthews doesn't want to go to the party at the day centre.	
c	Ms Matthews thinks she has put on weight.	
d	Ms Matthews decides to wear the blue dress and her black jacket.	
e	Ms Matthews wants to wear her mother's favourite perfume.	

6 Now correct the false statements in 5.

7 2.2 **Re-order the words below to form Polly's questions. Then listen and check.**

- **a** What / like / today? / to wear / would you
- **b** What / dress? / about / red / the
- **c** Do you / new perfume? / wear / your / want to
- **d** Which / put on? / shoes / want to / do you

8 Look at the pictures below. Use the structures in 7 to write four or five more questions. Then practise saying them aloud.

Talking about bodily functions

1 Use the verbs in the boxes to form expressions for bodily functions. (There may be more than one answer.)

be	do	go for	go to	have	throw	pass

Formal		Informal		Very informal/rude	
a b	*have* / ______ a bowel movement ______ a motion	g h	______ the toilet ______ a poo	o	______ a shit
c.	______ diarrhoea	i	______ the runs	p	______ the shits
d	______ constipated	j	______ bunged up	q	______ a piss
e	urinate / ______ water	k l m	______ the toilet go for/______ a pee ______ problems with the waterworks	r	to puke up
f	vomit	n	______up / ______ sick		

NB: We don't advise you to use very informal/rude expressions. However, it's important to understand service users when they use these expressions.

2 Re-order the words to form carers' questions.

a you had a poo? / When / was / the last time

b for you / a motion? / to pass / Is it difficult

c feeling / Are / constipated? / you still

d been / sick / have you / today? / How often

e your waterworks? / having problems / Are you / with

Assisting with toileting

1 Here are some guidelines for assisting with toileting. Add three or four more points.

- Ask the service user how much assistance they need.
- Avoid other people hearing when you discuss toileting issues.
- Make sure the door or curtains are closed.

2 Read about service user Anil Hoque. What does his carer, Rashid, need to consider when assisting with Mr Hoque's toileting?

eg *Mr Hoque's religious beliefs*

Anil Hoque (79) is a devout Muslim, born and raised in Bangladesh. He came to work in the UK when he was 23. He lives in a four-bedroom house in East London with his wife, son and daughter-in-law and their three children. He is a proud man and very private. He often finds it hard to accept or ask for help. He suffers from severe arthritis and finds it difficult to walk. He needs support three times a day from a carer to carry out personal care tasks.

3 2.5 **Listen to Part 1 and answer these questions.**

a What is Mr Hoque's daughter-in-law doing when Rashid arrives?

b Why does Mr Hoque want assistance?

c How does Rashid respect Mr Hoque's privacy? (two points)

4 🔊 2.5 **Use the words from the boxes to complete Rashid's expressions. Then listen to Part 2 and check your answers.**

~~close~~	change	fill up	loosen	put on	take	wait	wash

a Just let me *close* the door.
b I'm going to ______ my hands first, and ______ my apron.
c Now, would you like me to help you ______ your trousers and ______ them down, Mr Hoque?
d I'm just going to ______ your incontinence pad.
e I'm going to ______the bodna so you can wash yourself.
f I'll just ______ outside the door.

5 🔊 2.5 **Listen to Part 3 and answer these questions.**

a How does Rashid respect Mr Hoque's privacy?

b How does Rashid try to reduce Mr Hoque's embarrassment?

c How does Rashid encourage Mr Hoque to be independent?

6 Look at these sentences and write either 'O' (offering help) or 'R' (requesting help).

a	Would you like me to help you with your hair?	*O*
b	Can you take me back to the lounge, please?	
c	Do you need any help to brush your teeth?	
d	Could you come back and help me now, please?	
e	Do you want me to help you get dressed this morning?	

7 **Look at transcript 2.5 online. Find one or two more examples of offering and requesting help.**

8 🔊 2.6 **Listen and repeat what you hear, using the same intonation pattern as you speak.**

a Would you like me to help you with your hair?

b Do you need any help to brush your teeth?

c Do you want me to help you get dressed this morning?

d How can I help you this morning?

e Would you like me to help you loosen your trousers and take them down?

f Would you like any help to clean and dry the genital area?

Medical focus: Urinary tract infections (UTIs)

1 🔊 2.7 **Look at the diagram and repeat the medical terms you hear.**

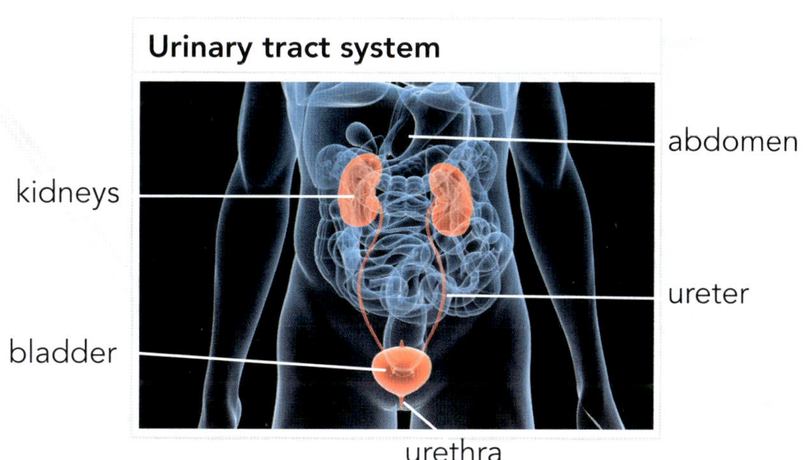

2 Complete the text below with the words in the boxes.

~~abdomen~~	bladder	blood	kidneys	penis
ureters	urethra	urine (x2)	vagina	waste

The kidneys, located on each side of the **(a)** *abdomen*, are the organs that filter **(b)** ________ from the blood. Waste fluid, or **(c)** ________, drains from the **(d)** ________ through tubes called **(e)** ________ into the **(f)** ________. When the bladder is full, this signals the need to go to the toilet. The **(g)** ________ then travels through the **(h)** ________ which is the opening in the genital area – **(i)** ________ or **(j)** ________ – where the waste fluid passes out of the body.

3 As you read the next part of the text, complete the sentences with these statements:

a transferred from the bowel to the bladder	**e** service users with recurring infections
b frequent need to use the toilet.	**f** cancer treatment, diabetes or constipation.
c following a prolapse of the vagina or womb,	**g** older men, an enlarged prostate
d nausea, vomiting and back pain.	**h** ~~are frequent, especially in women~~

Introduction

Urinary Tract Infections (UTIs) are common in elderly service users. Roughly three in 100 men in their 60s, and one in 10 in their 80s, will have a urinary infection. Repeat infections **(1)** *are frequent, especially in women.*

Causes

UTIs are often caused by bacteria **(2)** ____________________ via the urethra. Women have a greater risk of infection as the urethra is situated close to the anus. There is an increased risk in older women, **(3)** ____________________, or after the menopause when the skin around the genital area becomes more fragile. In **(4)** ____________________ means bacteria can collect in the bladder and cause infection. Other causes include a poor immune system due to (5) ____________________.

Symptoms

An infection of the bladder (cystitis) causes pain when passing urine and the **(6)** ____________________. Other symptoms include cloudy, bloody or smelly urine, abdominal pain or a high temperature. In more severe cases, such as kidney infection, symptoms also include feelings of **(7)** ____________________.

Treatment

Many UTIs can be treated with antibiotics, but **(8)** ____________________ should seek medical advice.

4 Re-order the sentences to form questions carers can use to ask about possible UTIs.

a you're having? / Can you / about the problems / tell me

b when you / Does it hurt / pass urine?

c Do you / frequently? / pass urine / have to

d any other / Do you / symptoms? / have

5 Write three or four pieces of advice for a new carer about how to prevent UTIs.

eg *Wipe your service user from front to back.*

Report writing (1)

1 What is your experience of writing reports in English or in your job? Give yourself a mark from 1 to 3.

Rating: 1 = confident, 2 = needs improvement, 3 = weak

What are your concerns? For example, are you worried about your writing style, your spelling or your use of grammatical structures?

2 What is the aim of the Daily Care Report? Tick (✓) the statements that are true.

a To communicate with service users.

b To communicate with colleagues.

c To record actions carried out with the service user.

d To record factual information about the visit.

3 Complete Polly's Daily Care Report for Irene Matthews using the words in the boxes.

bathroom	breakfast	clothes	daughter	hair	lively	mood	slept

Daily Care Report		*SunnyView* CARE	
Date am/pm	**Observations** *(please include information such as personal care given, food eaten, general mood and state of service user etc.)*	**Name of carer**	**Signature of carer**
14.05.16 am	Ms Matthews seemed quite (a) ___________ when I arrived this morning. I asked her about her evening. She told me her (b) ___________, Megan, had been round and they'd watched the final of Strictly Come Dancing together. She had (c) ___________ well. I got Ms Matthews out of bed, and she requested help to shower and wash her (d) ___________. Her mobility was normal. She explained there was a party at the day centre, so I helped her choose suitable day (e) ___________. She then asked for some (f) ___________ which I prepared – cereal, toast and jam – and she ate. We talked about the upcoming party at the day centre. Pavel – Ms Matthews has written a shopping list. Could you please collect her shopping? Thanks. (g) ___________, kitchen and living room cleaned and tidied. I left Ms Matthews in a good (h) ___________. The taxi arrived to take her to the day centre as I was leaving.	Polly Simpson	P Simpson

4 Put the following sentences taken from Polly's report under the correct category.

Mood	Physical state	Develop/ maintain rapport	Actions and justifications	Internal communication	Follow-up tasks
		1			

1 ~~We talked about the upcoming party at the day centre~~.

2 Bathroom, kitchen and living room cleaned and tidied.

3 She had slept well.

4 Ms Matthews seemed quite lively when I arrived this morning.

5 I got Ms Matthews out of bed, and she requested help to shower and wash her hair.

6 Pavel – Ms Matthews has written a shopping list. Could you please collect her shopping? Thanks.

5 Read Polly's report again and write down some more examples for each category in 4.

Unit 3

Food and nutrition

Target areas

• Food and drink items • Using adapted utensils • Providing active support at mealtimes • Using encouragement and praise • Completing a nutrition chart • Medical focus: Type 2 diabetes • Simple past review • Study skills (1): Strategies for reading

In their shoes

1 Read these statistics and write two or three reasons for malnutrition among elderly service users.

- Three million people in the UK are malnourished or at risk of malnutrition.
- Malnutrition includes under-nutrition (insufficient food intake) and over-nutrition (excessive food intake).
- 10% of older people suffer from malnutrition.
- 30% of older people admitted to hospital are malnourished.

(Social Care Institute for Excellence and The Patients Association, 2011)

2 Look at the pictures and answer the questions that follow.

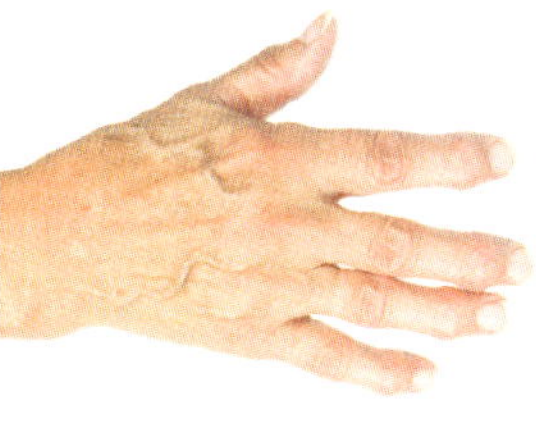

a Why might it be difficult for these service users to eat and drink independently?

b Think of other situations where a service user may need assistance or encouragement to eat.

c How can carers assist service users in these situations?

3 Here are some guidelines for supporting service users in eating and drinking. Add three or four more points.

- Give the service user the opportunity to wash their hands if they wish.
- Put on your PPE.

Food and drink items

1 Look at the nutrition plate and label as many items as you can in 60 seconds.

2 Look at the food items in 1 and find:

a Two items you should eat only occasionally and two items you can eat any time.

b Three or four items that cause allergies in some people.

c Two items of each of the following: food high in saturated fat, food low in carbohydrates and food high in protein.

3 Match the following definitions to the correct dietary preferences.

a	A diet excluding alcohol and pork where meat and dairy products are prepared according to Islamic law.	pescetarian
b	A diet excluding pork and shellfish and where meat and dairy products are prepared according to Jewish law.	vegan
c	A diet based on fish products and excluding meat.	vegetarian
d	A diet excluding all meat, dairy and fish products.	gluten-free
e	A diet excluding wheat, barley and rye products which cause an allergic reaction in some people.	kosher
f	A diet excluding meat and fish, but including dairy products.	halal

4 Do you have experience of service users who follow a special diet? How do you make sure their preferences are respected? What things do you have to be careful about?

Using adapted utensils

1 Label the adapted utensils with the words in the boxes.

adapted cutlery ~~two-handled mug~~ insulated bowl non-slip mat plate guard

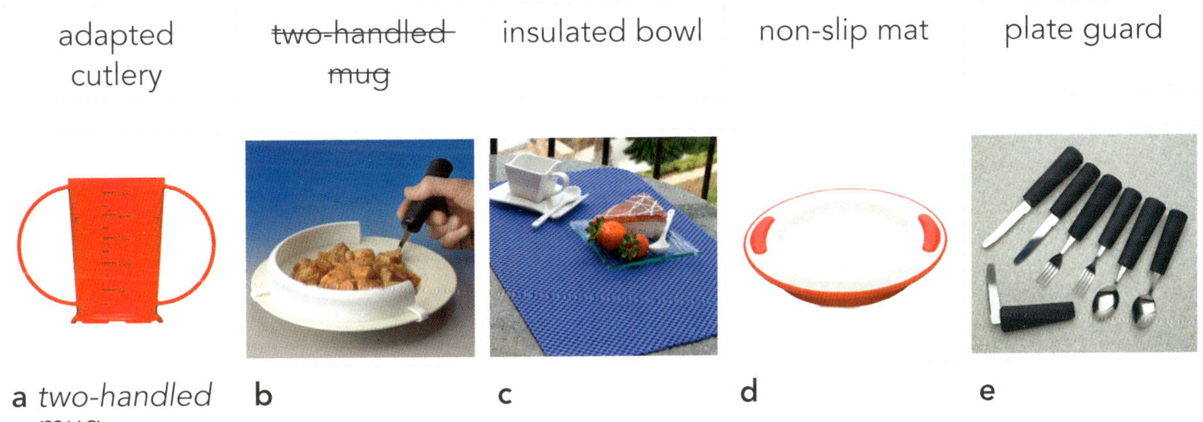

a *two-handled mug* b c d e

Images used with permission from Welcome Mobility. www.welcomemobility.co.uk

2 Read about service user, Martha McDonald. How easy do you think it will it be for Martha to learn to use adapted utensils?

Martha McDonald (75) has been diagnosed with severe arthritis, which has recently spread to her hands. She finds it more and more difficult to grip cutlery while eating. Consequently, she has been recommended to buy some adapted utensils. Her carer, Josie, has agreed to help Martha start using the utensils.

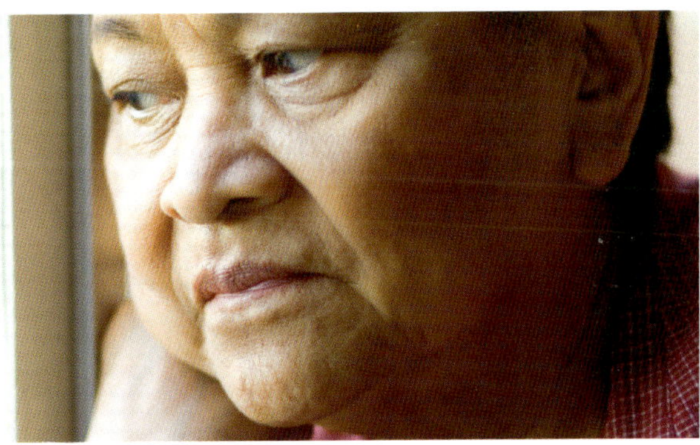

3 🔊 3.1 **Listen to Josie assisting Martha and tick (✓) the utensil(s) she uses.**

a non-slip mat		**b** insulated bowl		**c** adapted cutlery		**d** plate guard	

4 Write *T* (true) or *F* (false) for each statement. Then correct the false statements.

a	Martha has never used the adapted spoon before.	*T*
b	Josie shows Martha how to use the utensils.	
c	Martha succeeds first time.	
d	Josie encourages Martha to try again.	

5 🔊 3.1 **Listen again. Complete Josie's description of the adapted utensils in 1.**

a *non-slip mat*: It'll ______________________________ around.

b *adapted spoon*: The padded handles will ____________________.

6 Re-order the words to form more descriptions. Then write the correct utensil from 1 for each.

a It / spilling / will stop / from / your food __________

b It / if you need longer / your / food hot / will keep / to eat __________

c easier / The handles / make it / will / to hold __________

7 🔊 3.1 **Use the verbs in the boxes to complete the instructions for using the adapted utensils. Listen and check your answers.**

hold	push (x2)	grip (x2)

a You _______ the spoon like this in your right hand.

b You_______ the food towards the plate guard and then _______ it onto your spoon.

c You don't need to _______ it so tightly.

d Try again, but this time just _______ it a tiny bit harder.

8 Practise describing and explaining how to use the adapted utensils in 1 (p41) to a service user.

Providing active support at meal times

1 Write two or three situations where carers need to provide more active support at meal times.

eg *The service user has had an accident and has reduced use of their arms.*

2 Match the two halves to complete guidelines for providing active support at meal times.

a	Help the service user into → 7		1	in the same mouthful.
b	Sit in front of the service user,		2	to chew and swallow each mouthful.
c	Provide the		3	don't draw attention to it.
d	Give the service user enough time		4	the service user as they eat.
e	Don't mix food and drink		5	service user with a napkin.
f	Don't rush the service user or		6	give the next spoonful before he/ she is ready.
g	If the service user spills food or drink,		7	a comfortable position in preparation for eating.
h	Chat with		8	slightly to the side.

3 Give a reason for the guidelines in *g* and *h* above.

4 Read about service user Filuck. How do you think Filuck and his carer, Robert, communicate with each other?

Filuck (57) has had a stroke and has difficulty feeding himself. Due to the nature of his stroke, Filuck finds speaking extremely difficult.

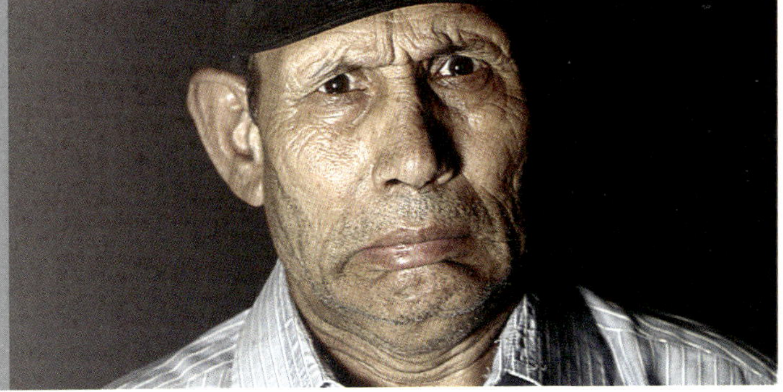

5 🔊 3.2 **Listen to the conversation between Filuck and Robert. Read the stage directions eg [*Smiles and ...*], as you listen.**

6 🔊 3.2 **Take the role of Robert. Use the stage directions to practise the non-verbal communication with Filuck as you support him.**

Using encouragement and praise

1 🔊 3.3 **Rashid is preparing dinner for Mr Hoque. Listen to Part 1 and answer these questions.**

a Why was Mr Hoque reluctant to eat dinner today?

b When did he last eat a proper meal?

c What did Mr Hoque finally choose to eat?

2 🔊 3.3 **Listen to Part 2. Add vowels (*a, e, i, o, u*) to complete Rashid's expressions.**

a You're d__ __ng w__ll. *P*

b C__ __ld y__ __ j__st try a l__ttl__ m__r__? ________

c Th__t's g__ __d. ________

d Y__ __'v__ d__n__ w__ll. ________

3 Look at the expressions in 2. Write *E* if Rashid encourages Mr Hoque and *P* if he praises him.

4 🔊 3.4 **Listen to Rashid talking to Mr Hoque. Notice how he uses intonation to make his voice sound friendly and caring. Practise giving encouragement and praise using the same intonation.**

Grammar focus: Past simple review

1 You were introduced to service user Irene Matthews in Unit 2. What do you remember about her?

eg *She's 87 years old.*

2 3.5 **Carer Polly is assisting Ms Matthews. Listen to Part 1 and answer these questions.**

a What medical condition does Ms Matthews suffer from?

b What does Ms Matthews decide to eat for breakfast?

c Why can't Ms Matthews have her first choice?

3 3.5 **Listen to Part 2. How does Polly encourage Ms Matthews to be independent?**

4 Read how we use the past simple to talk about the past.

Use the **past simple** to talk about actions that started and finished in the past.	*I **arrived** at around 8.15 this morning.* (regular verb) *Daisy **chatted** about her evening.* (regular verb: notice the spelling) *Michael **ate** toast and cereal for breakfast.* (irregular verb) *What time **did** you **go** to bed last night?* (question)

5 3.6 **Underline the correct verb tense to complete the sentences. Listen and check your answers.**

Ms M: I *test* / *<u>tested</u>* my glucose level before you *arrive* / *arrived* and it *is* / *was* high: 14.2.

Polly: Lots of people with Type 2 diabetes *have* / *had* quite high blood glucose levels in the morning.

Ms M: Yes, the nurse *tell* / *told* me to be careful.

Polly: I *go* / *went* on a training course recently in food and nutrition. I *learn* / *learnt* that people with diabetes need to watch what they eat, especially in the mornings.

6 3.7 **Write the following verbs in the past simple. Listen and check your answers.**

a arrive	**b** ask	**c** be	**d** chat	**e** decide	**f** help	**g** sit	**h** take
arrived							

7 3.8 **All regular past simple verbs end in *-ed*, but this ending can be pronounced in three different ways. Listen to how we pronounce the past tense forms *watched, listened* and *decided.***

8 3.9 **Now listen to some more verbs. Do they sound like *watched, listened* or *decided*? Write them in the correct column. Then practise saying them aloud.**

watched	listened	decided

9 Complete the Daily Care Report for Irene Matthews. Use verbs from 6.

Daily Care Report		SunnyView CARE	
Date am/pm	**Observations** *(please include information such as personal care given, food eaten, general mood and state of service user etc.)*	**Name of carer**	**Signature of carer**
15.05.16 am	When I (a) arrived Ms Matthews (b) ___ bright and cheery. She (c) ___ a shower and then I (d) ___ her to choose something for breakfast. Her blood sugar level (e) ___ high at 14.2, so she (f) ___ to have cereal, semi-skimmed milk and tea. Then Ms Matthews (g) ___ me prepare the meal. After breakfast we sat and (h) ___ about her grandchildren's upcoming visit on Sunday.	Polly Simpson	P Simpson

Medical focus: Type 2 diabetes

1 What do you already know about Type 2 diabetes? Do you think these statements are *T* (true) or *F* (false)?

a	Eating sweets and sugar does not cause diabetes.	T
b	This condition only occurs in adults.	
c	Type 2 diabetes is the most common form of diabetes.	
d	People of South Asian origin are at higher risk of diabetes.	
e	Type 2 diabetes is very easy to detect.	

2 Read the text and check your answers to 1.

Type 2 diabetes

There are currently 2.8 million people with diabetes in the UK, of whom 85% suffer from Type 2 diabetes. The condition first appears generally at around the age of 40, and particularly at risk are people who are obese (where it can arise much earlier, even in children) or have a family history of the condition. Type 2 diabetes is most common in people of African-Caribbean, Middle Eastern or South Asian origin.

This condition develops when the pancreas fails to produce enough of the hormone insulin, which controls sugar (glucose) levels in the blood. Sugar consumption can contribute to developing Type 2 diabetes, but it is not a cause. The main symptoms of this condition are frequent urination, feelings of thirst and tiredness and blurred vision, as well as unexplained loss of weight and itching around the genital area.

When blood glucose levels are low, either from too much medication, too much exercise or too little food, this causes hypoglycaemia or a 'hypo'. It is important to treat a hypo immediately, otherwise the diabetic can lose consciousness or begin fitting.

Type 2 diabetes develops slowly over time, and patients may not realise they are diabetic. However, the symptoms can be relieved once the diabetes is treated and under control.

3 Correct the false statements in 1.

4 Now answer these questions. Go online, if necessary.

a How can diabetic service users control their Type 2 diabetes?

b What other health issues is Type 2 diabetes associated with?

c How can you help treat a service user experiencing a hypo?

5 Write four or five pieces of nutritional advice to give a service user recently diagnosed with Type 2 diabetes.

eg *Eat three meals a day.*

6 Practise offering the advice in question 5 to a service user. Begin with these expressions:

- *It's a good idea to …*
- *You should … It's really important that you … It's better to …*

Study skills (1): Strategies for reading

1 We read for different reasons. Tick (✓) the answers that apply for you.

	I read ... in English	Often	Sometimes	Rarely
a	personal emails, Facebook messages etc.			
b	newspapers and magazines (paper or online)			
c	novels (paper or e-books)			
d	professional correspondence (email, letters)			
e	reference books and articles about social care (paper or e-books)			

2 Write down three or four things that make it difficult for you to read in English.

eg *unfamiliar vocabulary*

3 Read this advice from other social carers on how to increase your reading speed. Which do you think are helpful?

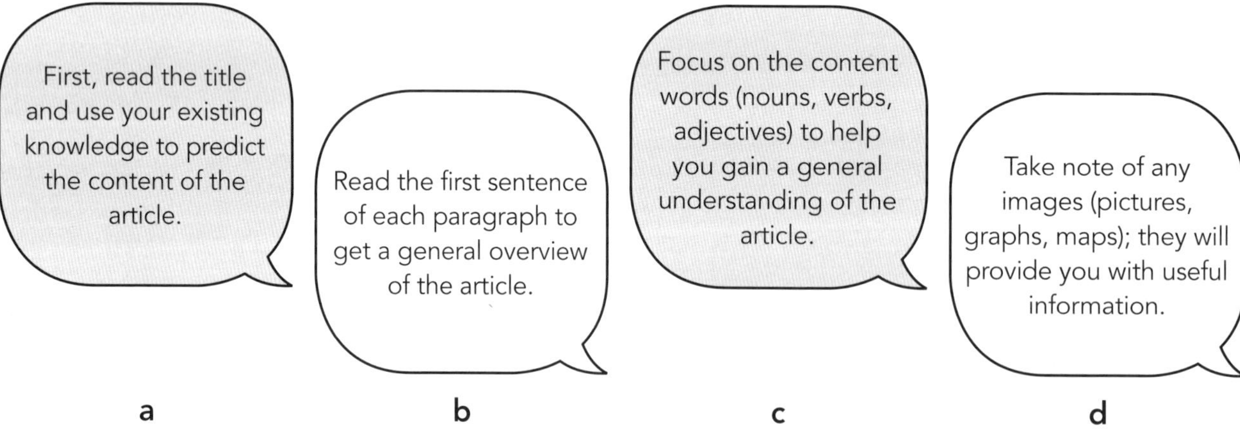

4 Look at this technique for reading. Label it with the subheadings in the boxes.

Review	Read	Recall

Reading technique

(a) ________

Read the title and/or introduction and form questions about the article. Read the first section with these questions in your mind. Look for answers in the text and write more questions if necessary.

(b) ________

After each section think about your questions. Can you answer the questions from memory? If not, look back at the text. Do this as often as you need to. NB: You may not be able to answer all of your questions.

(c) ________

Once you've finished the chapter or article, answer all the questions again. If you can't, look back and refresh your memory.

5 Use the techniques in 3 and 4 when reading this article about malnutrition.

Malnutrition in the community

Malnutrition (under-nourishment and over-nourishment) in the community is the result of many different factors. People with severely reduced mobility as well as those who are housebound are most at risk. This is especially the case for those who don't have a support network to help with cooking and shopping. However, it is not only the elderly; those with chronic conditions are also at risk of malnutrition. It is also seasonal, with more people suffering malnutrition in the winter than the rest of the year.

High incidences of malnutrition in the community are caused by limited or badly organised services. This is often the situation faced by patients following discharge from hospital. Patients sometimes fail to receive the key support services they need, such as home help or meals on wheels. They might be discharged and become isolated, with no social care support provided.

The UK has an ageing population. By 2034 it is expected that 23% of the population will be 65 or more. According to the European Nutrition for Health Alliance (ENHA), malnutrition is endemic in the community. As such, the ENHA has indicated that social carers should be more vigilant in identifying and treating service users at risk from malnutrition.

Adapted from *Malnutrition in the Community and Hospital Setting*, The Patients Association (2011)

6 Reflect on the reading process in 5.

a Did you find that the techniques you used made it easier to read and understand the article? Why (not)?

b What do you plan to do differently next time you read an article in English?

7 When you read about a new service user, use these simple question words to help you understand the information: *Who? What? When? How?* Now use this strategy to read the following case study. Write notes in the table as you read.

John (25) has mild learning disabilities and lives on his own in a supported living project. He is supported on a daily basis by social care worker Tanzilla (23), who lives locally. Tanzilla visits John for one hour a day to help him plan all aspects of his daily living, including giving support with buying his shopping and answering his correspondence.

Tanzilla has recently become aware that John may not be eating a particularly healthy diet, preferring to snack on crisps, chocolate, ice cream and sandwiches. Tanzilla understands that she must respect John's decisions and must not force her own standards upon him. However, she is worried that if she does not intervene, John could develop short-term and long-term health-related problems.

Who?	
What?	
When?	
How?	

8 Answer the following questions and then check the answers online.

a List three or four health conditions that John might experience as a result of his unhealthy eating habits.

b Write advice for Tanzilla to give John on healthy eating etc.

Unit 4

Manual handling

Target areas

• Equipment for manual handling • Giving clear, friendly instructions • Encouraging a service user to participate actively • Medical focus: Pressure ulcers • Asking for assistance •Report writing (2)

In their shoes

1 Read the following quote and think about two service users (or elderly people) you know. How might the manual handling process differ between them?

'It is important to remember that no two lifts are the same. This is to do with the person, their mood or just how they are feeling on that particular day.'

2 Rate your ability to carry out the manual handling process effectively in English.

Rating: 1 = confident, 2 = needs improvement, 3 = weak

a I am able to put the service user at ease.

b I am able to give the service user clear, simple instructions in a friendly manner.

c I am able to explain my actions to the service user and avoid confusion.

Equipment for manual handling

1 Label the pieces of equipment used for manual handling.

sling hoist	handling belt	lifting cushion	slide sheets	support rails	transfer board

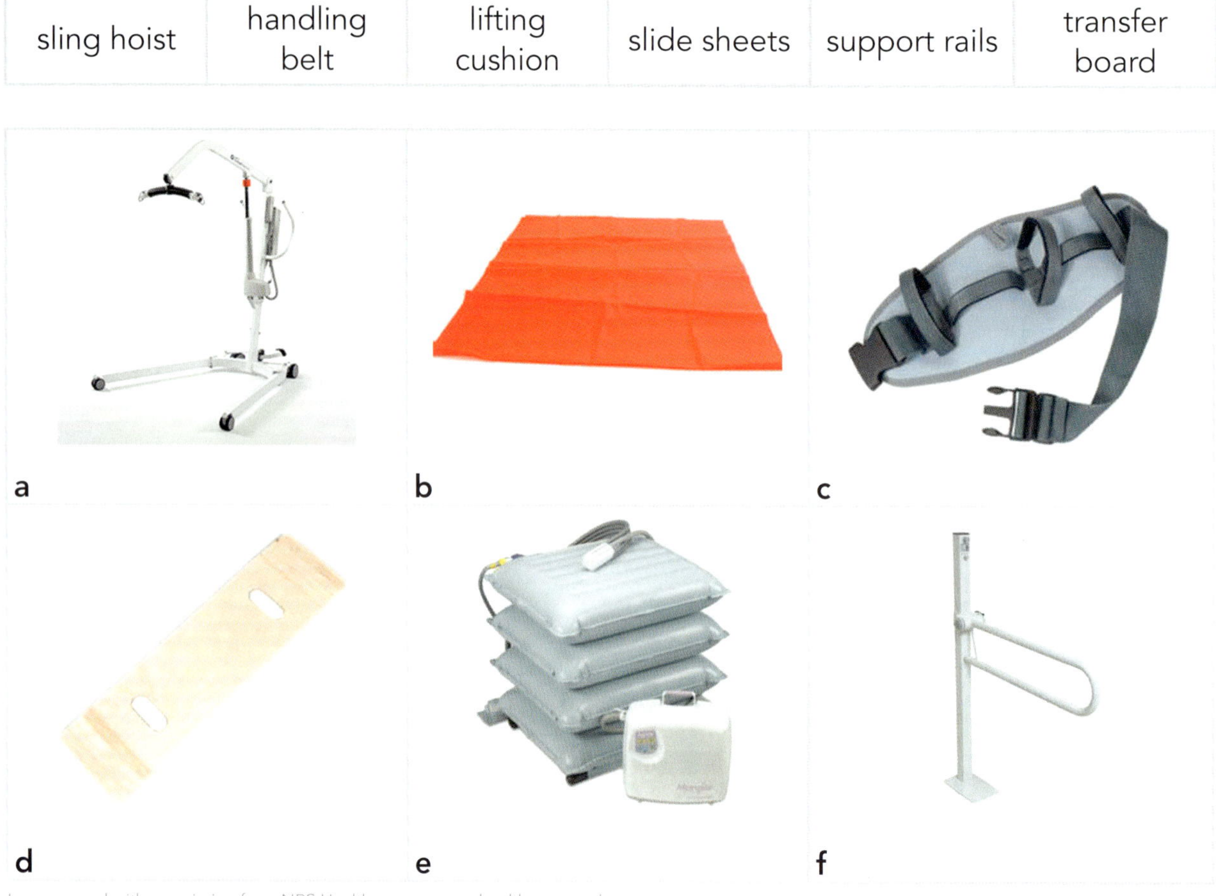

a b c d e f

Images used with permission from NRS Healthcare. www.nrshealthcare.co.uk

2 4.1 **Listen and complete the carers' explanations. Then choose the correct name for each piece of equipment from 1.**

a **We can use it to** help you move *from your wheelchair to the toilet*. *transfer board*

b **It can be used to** help____________________. __________.

c **It's for** lifting you ____________________. __________.

d **It's to** help ____________________. __________.

e **You can use them to** support yourself as ____________________. __________.

f **It's used to** help ____________________. __________.

3 Use the structures (in bold) in 2 and practise explaining the equipment to service users.

eg *It's to support … / You can use it to support …*

Giving clear, friendly instructions

1 Read about service user Marina Staples. What problems does Marina have with mobility?

Marina Staples (78) lives in a residential care home. She has severe arthritis in her legs, so she finds it difficult to walk at certain times and hard to get out of furniture (eg her bed and chair). The doctor has told her to walk whenever possible with the aid of a walking frame. Her carers have been instructed by Marina's GP and social worker to help and encourage her to use the frame, especially when walking short distances eg from the dining room to her bedroom.

2 Write down three or four movements Marina might make to get out of bed. Use a dictionary if necessary.

eg *sit up, bend her leg*

3 🔊 4.2 **Rosie is Marina's carer. Number her instructions in the correct order (1–7). Then listen and check your answers.**

a	Straighten up slowly. Push the walking frame forward.	
b	Now sit on the edge of the bed.	
c	Bend your foot and lift your heel.	
d	Hold onto the walking frame.	
e	Can you roll over to your right side?	*1*
f	Lift up your leg. Now the other one.	
g	Put your weight on your left leg first. Now your right leg.	

4 Look at these different ways to give friendly instructions. Rewrite Rosie's instructions in 3 and make them more friendly.

- Can you bend your knee?
- Could you just bend your knee?
- Can you just bend you knee for me?

NB:

- When you ask *Can you do it* ***for me?*** you create a bond with your service user. It shows him/her you are working together to achieve the desired result (eg *bend your knee*).
- You can use the word *just* to show that a procedure (eg *bend your knee*) won't be too difficult or too painful.

5 **Look at the pictures below. For each one, write two or three instructions about moving that the carer might give to the service user. Check your answers online.**

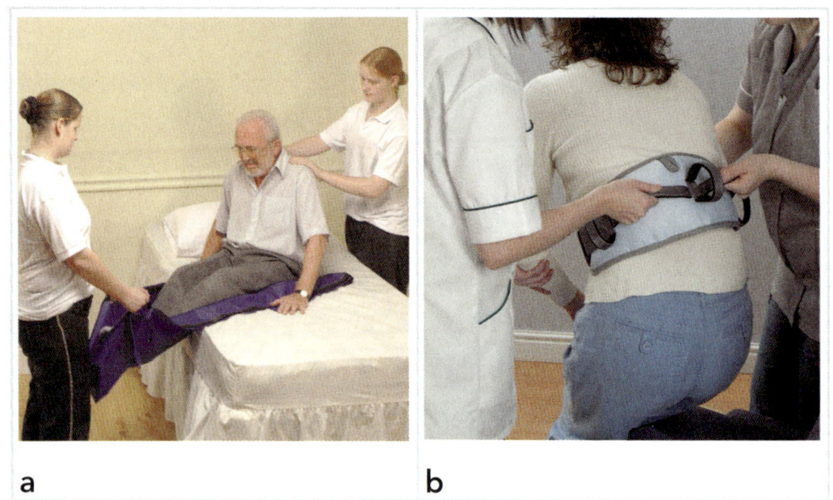

Images used with permission from Home & Medical. www.homeandmedical.co.uk

eg **a** *Bend your knee.*

6 **Practise giving the instructions in 4 and 5.**

7 4.3 **Listen to two carers giving the same instruction. Which carer sounds more friendly, carer 1 or carer 2? What happens to this carer's voice?**

8 4.4 **Listen to how Rosie gives instructions. Notice that the tone of her voice goes up and down. This makes her sound friendly and caring. Copy her intonation pattern to give the following instructions.**

- a Could you roll over to your right side?
- b Now can you just sit on the edge of the bed?
- c Can you hold onto the walking frame?
- d Could you just put your weight on your left leg first? Now your right leg.
- e Can you just straighten up slowly for me? Push the walking frame forward.
- f Could you bend your foot and lift your heel for me?
- g Can you lift up your leg for me? Now the other one.

9 **Carers need to keep checking that the service user is comfortable as they transfer them. Add vowels (*a, e, i, o, u*) to complete these carers' questions. When do the carers ask these questions? Tick (✓) the correct column.**

		Before transfer	During transfer	After transfer
a	Are you c_mf_rtable, or d_ y_u need me to re-p_sition y_u?			✓
b	_re you re_dy to tr_nsfer?			
c	Are th_re any pr_ssure ar_as I n_ed to consid_r b_fore I mov_ you?			
d	Is _v_rything _K?			
e	_re you in _ny p_in?			

10 🔊 4.5 **It is also important to keep the service user informed as you carry out a transfer. Re-order these words to form what the carer says. Then listen and check.**

a stand up / I'm / to / going / help you

b transfer / into your wheelchair / going to / We're / you

c for you / the frame / He's / to hold / just going

d going to lift / They're / you up onto your bed / just

Risk assessment for manual handling

1 Read the district nurse's risk assessment for Marina. Answer these questions:

a What is the district nurse's physical assessment of Marina?

b What advice does the district nurse give about handling equipment?

c What do Marina's carers also need to be aware of when they transfer her?

Manual Handling Risk Assessment

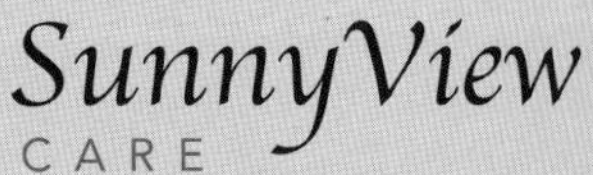

Name: Marina Staples

District Nurse: Jacqueline Roberts

Body Build: Average

Problems: Reluctant to walk around residential home. Prefers to use wheelchair.

Handling constraints: Weakness and pain in both legs. This can result in Marina becoming uncooperative and upset and not wanting to walk. She then wants to use her wheelchair, which in turn will decrease her mobility and independence.

Tasks: Walking around the home. Also sitting and standing from the bed and the toilet.

Methods to be used: Carer to encourage Marina to walk with her frame whenever possible and to avoid the use of the wheelchair as this will decrease her mobility. Carers may use a handling belt to help Marina get on her feet and onto her walking frame. Carers should not attempt to lift Marina to her feet without the use of the handling belt as this could result in injury to both Marina and carer. Marina should be praised when she walks using her frame, and the carer should walk beside her and be ready to offer assistance should she become tired and need to sit down.

Any remaining problems: Marina does not always want to use her frame and may get upset and raise her voice at carers. It is important for carers to be supportive and encouraging whenever possible and to praise Marina when she uses her frame.

Date: 21/06/2015.

Assessor: Jacqueline Roberts.

Review Date: 20/07/2016.

2 4.6 **Rosie is transferring Marina. Listen to Part 1. Write *T* (true) or *F* (false) for each statement.**

a Marina would prefer to use her wheelchair today.

b Marina's GP has advised her not to exercise.

c Marina accepts Rosie's compromise.

3 4.6 **Listen to Part 2. Describe Marina's journey from her bedroom to the dining room.**

eg *First, Marina tries to stand using her ...*

4 Match the two halves to form Rosie's instructions. Listen to Part 2 again and check your answers.

a	Put your hands on the frame → 3	1	a bit more slowly.
b	We'll stand up on	2	if you need to.
c	Now grip your walking	3	and push yourself up off the bed.
d	Stop and rest	4	the count of three.
e	Marina, just take it	5	frame with both hands.

Encouraging a service user to participate actively

1 Read Rosie's reflective journal. How might Rosie encourage Marina to participate more actively in the handling process?

eg *She could try to build up Marina's confidence.*

SunnyView TRAINING

What have I learnt?	What happened when I put this into practice?
Sometimes it seems quicker and easier for me (and Marina) if I carry out the transfer myself. My supervisor suggested we encourage Marina to be more independent, especially when we are manoeuvring her.	I was surprised at the difference in Marina. She's suddenly much more independent, and she can actually do a lot more by herself than I thought.

2 4.7 **Add the vowels to complete Rosie's expressions for encouraging and praising Marina. Then listen and check your answers.**

a	Take y_ _r t_m_.	c	Th_t's _t.
b	Y_ _'re d_ _ng v_ry w_ll.	d	W_ll d_n_.

3 Read the guidelines below for transferring service users and match them to one of the expressions a to e.

Guidelines for Transferring Service Users	SunnyView CARE
Explore the service user's concerns.	*You look a little worried.*
Empathise with the service user.	
Explain the reason for the transfer.	
Try to reach a shared decision with the service user.	
Support the service user.	

a	Sometimes it feels a bit overwhelming.
b	I'm here with you.
c	Why don't you try using the support rails to help you?
d	~~You look a little worried~~.
e	You need to move around more.

4 Read the following conversation and find one or two more examples for each guideline in 3.

Rosie: Are you ready for lunch, Marina?

Marina: Yes, my dear.

Rosie: Good. Let me get your walking frame for you.

Marina: Ooo, I don't know, love.

Rosie: You sound a bit unsure.

Marina: Can't you push me in the wheelchair today? I was in a lot of pain this morning.

Rosie: Well, it's important that you use your legs. The GP wants you to do as much exercise as possible. *[Silence]* I understand; it's not always easy. *[Silence]* How about you try using your frame? If it's too painful, I'll transfer you to your wheelchair. We'll do it together.

Marina: That sounds like a good compromise.

Grammar focus: Modals for polite requests

1 Read about service user Martin Cropper and answer the questions below.

Martin Cropper (39) has muscular dystrophy. He lives in supported accommodation and needs constant care. His carers, Robert and Amit, live locally and have been working together as a team for a year. They both have a very friendly and relaxed relationship with Martin. As part of their role, Robert and Amit often take Martin out to the pub, where he enjoys nothing more than a pint of lager and a bar meal!

a What daily tasks might Martin need support with?

b What handling equipment might the carers use to transfer Martin from his bed to the wheelchair?

2 4.8 Listen to Part 1. Underline the correct words in *italics* to complete the sentences.

a Martin is *excited about* / *worried about* / *tired of* going to the pub.

b Martin suggests they go to their *usual pub* / *a new pub* / *a restaurant.*

c Amit thinks The Royal Oak might be *busy* / *closed* / *expensive*.

d Robert usually has *a cooked breakfast* / *pie and mash* / *just a drink* at The Albert.

e Martin is in *a little pain* / *a lot of pain* / *no pain* today.

3 Read how we use *can, could* and *would you mind* to make polite requests.

Language for polite requests	
Can/could you + infinitive	Could you check the temperature of the water?
Would you mind + *ing*	Would you mind helping me transfer Mr Smith?
If you can/could + infinitive	If you can lift Marjorie's left leg.

4 4.8 Listen to Part 2 and complete Robert's requests.

a Would ______ mind ______ me the sling, please?

b ______ ______ could support Martin with your hand on his back and guide the hoist.

c Could ______ ______ hold onto the cross bar for me, please?

d ______ ______ ______ push Martin a bit more to the left, please?

e Keep ______ on for a moment, OK?

5 🔊 4.9 **Go to the transcript online. Take the role of Robert and practise carrying out the same transfer with Martin.**

6 **Write a dialogue between Amit and Robert as they use a slide sheet to move Martin. Use expressions from this unit and follow these steps:**

- Amit asks Robert for assistance to carry out a transfer with Martin.
  eg Amit: '*Excuse me, Robert, can you help me transfer Martin, please?*'
- Amit asks Robert to bring the slide sheet.
- Amit asks Martin if he is ready to transfer, then asks him to carry out certain movements to carry out the transfer.
- Robert offers encouragement as Martin carries out the movements.
- Amit asks Robert to pull the slide sheet under Martin and help position him safely on it.
- Amit explains the transfer is complete and asks Martin if he is comfortable.
- Amit thanks Robert for his help.

Medical focus: Pressure ulcers

1 **Match the terms (a–e) to the correct definition (1–5).**

a	superficial	1	outer layer of skin
b	epidermis	2	hole
c	dermis	3	skin (in this case) that is dying due to lack of blood supply
d	cavity	4	on or near the surface (of the skin)
e	tissue necrosis	5	deeper layer of skin

2 **As you read the following article about pressure ulcers, write notes to answer these questions.**

a How do service users develop pressure ulcers?

b Which service users are most likely to develop pressure sores?

c How can pressure ulcers be prevented?

Pressure ulcers

Around half a million people a year in the UK develop pressure ulcers, also known as 'pressure sores' or 'bedsores'. Those most at risk include the over-70s, diabetics and anyone experiencing mobility issues. Pressure ulcers develop when extra pressure stops the flow of blood to the skin, starving it of oxygen and nutrients. The skin then breaks down and a pressure ulcer forms.

There are four grades of pressure ulcer.

Grade one are superficial ulcers. The skin appears discoloured (red, purple or blue depending on skin type), but remains intact. The area may hurt or become itchy, warm or hard.

Grade two ulcers are where the epidermis or the dermis becomes damaged and the ulcer resembles an open wound.

Grade three ulcers are deep, cavity-like wounds with damage to the epidermis, dermis and the underlying tissue.

Grade four ulcers are those which can result in gangrene or blood poisoning.

An effective way to prevent pressure ulcers is to change positions regularly. In general, wheelchair users need to change positions every 15–30 minutes, and those confined to bed should change position every two hours. Once a pressure ulcer has developed, it is important to minimise any further pressure to enable it to heal. Good nutrition and giving up smoking can also help prevent pressure ulcers.

3 Mark 'X' on the body map where the following service users might suffer pressure ulcers:

a Someone who is confined to bed

b A wheelchair user

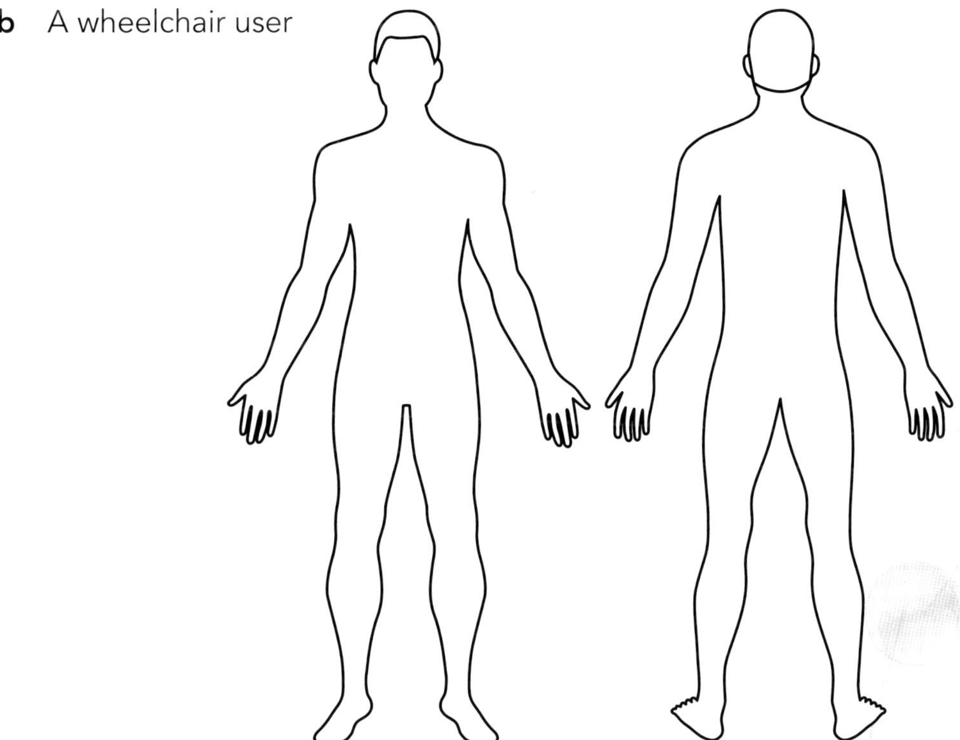

4 Advise your patient on a diet to prevent pressure sores. Use the food plate in Unit 3 (p40) and go online if necessary.

Report writing (2)

1 **We use conjunctions like *and, but, because* etc. to join phrases and sentences together. Conjunctions show the relationship between different ideas, and they make our reports easier to read. Read the following Daily Care Report for Annie and underline all the conjunctions.**

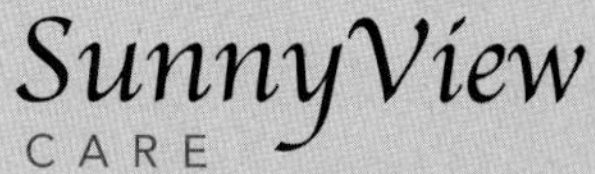

Annie was up when I arrived this morning. At first she seemed a little down, but her mood improved quickly. First, we chatted about her dentist's appointment today while we made a cup of tea together. The bed sheets were soaked through with urine, so I changed them and put the soaked ones onto a hot wash. (Gladys – can you hang them to dry when you come at 5.30? Thanks.) Annie requested a bath and I helped her to wash herself as she was very wet with urine. Then she put on her day clothes. Even though she wasn't very hungry, I convinced her to eat some toast. Medication dispensed, signed for and prompted. Bathroom and kitchen cleaned. At the end of the visit, Annie was in a much better mood. I left a message in her memory notebook in order to remind her that Gladys would be on tonight.

2 **Add the conjunctions from 1 to the table below. Add a few more, if possible.**

The writer wants to ...	Example	Conjunction
... add information	*in addition*	
... illustrate cause and effect	*because*	
... provide supporting information	*for example*	
... demonstrate an aim	*to*	
... offer a contrast	*however*	
... give a concession	*although*	
... show a sequence	*after*	*At first*

3 **Underline the correct conjunctions to complete the Daily Care Report for Martin.**

Daily Care Report		SunnyView CARE	
Date am/pm	**Observations** *(please include information such as personal care given, food eaten, general mood and state of service user etc.)*	**Name of carer**	**Signature of carer**
14.05.15 lunchtime	(a) When/Before we arrived this lunchtime, Martin was cheerful (b) and/but he was excited about our lunch date at the pub. (c) Then/Because we agreed on the choice of pub (d) as/in order to we carried out our duties. Martin was already dressed. (e) However/Although, we checked to see if he wanted to change into different clothes. We transferred Martin to his wheelchair using the sling and hoist (f) so that/and we could take him out.	Amit Singh	A Singh

Unit 5

Pain and medication

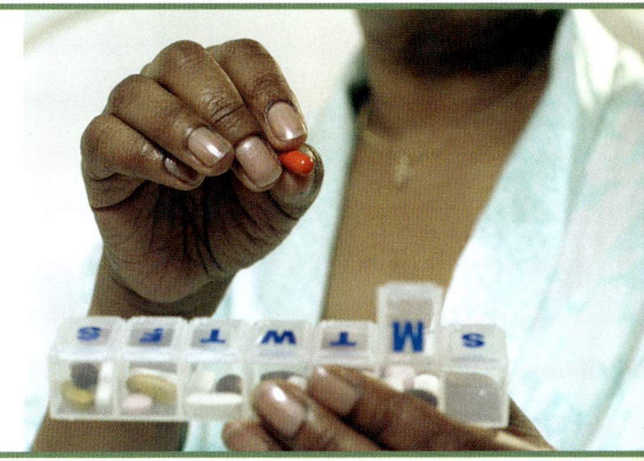

Target areas

• Monitoring dosages • Modals: may/might • Talking about side effects • Asking about pain • Medical focus: Stroke • Study skills (2): Recording and learning new vocabulary

In their shoes

1 How do you feel about taking medication? Read these comments. Which ones remind you of service users or people you know?

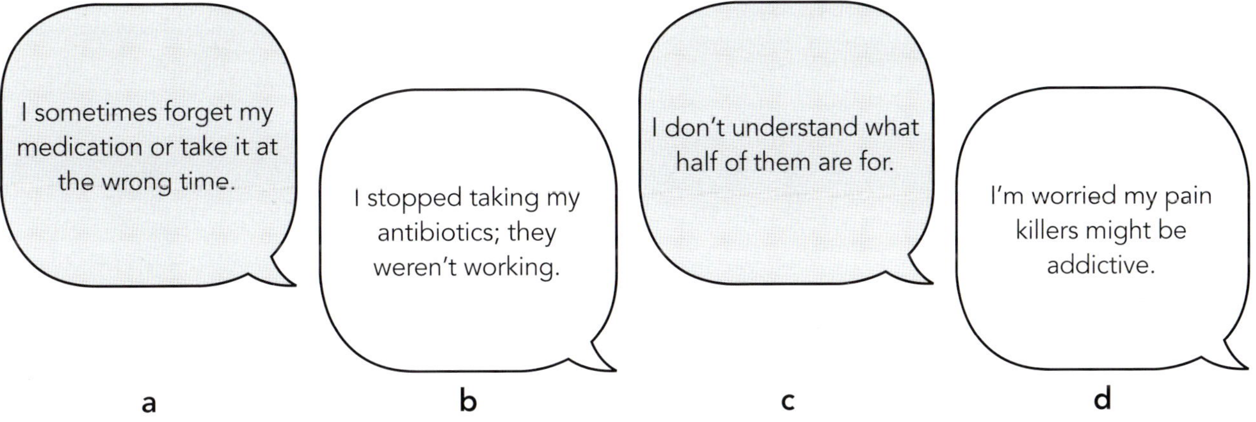

2 Now answer these questions.

a Why is it important for service users to understand their medication?

b What problems do some service users have when taking medication?

c What is the role of the carer regarding medication?

Monitoring dosages (forms, routes, frequency, quantity)

1 Read the Seven Rights of Medication. Why are they so important?

Seven Rights of Medication
1. Right service user
2. Right medication
3. Right dose (quantity)
4. Right route (eg by mouth)
5. Right time
6. Right form (eg *tablet*)
7. Right outcome (result)

NB: The word 'drug' sometimes has a negative meaning. It's better to say *medication* or *medicine*.

2 The pictures below show different forms of medication. Label them with the words in the boxes.

tablet and capsule	cream/ ointment	drops	inhaler	~~injection~~
IV drip	patch	syrup	spray	suppository

a. *injection*	**b.**	**c.**	**d.**	**e.**

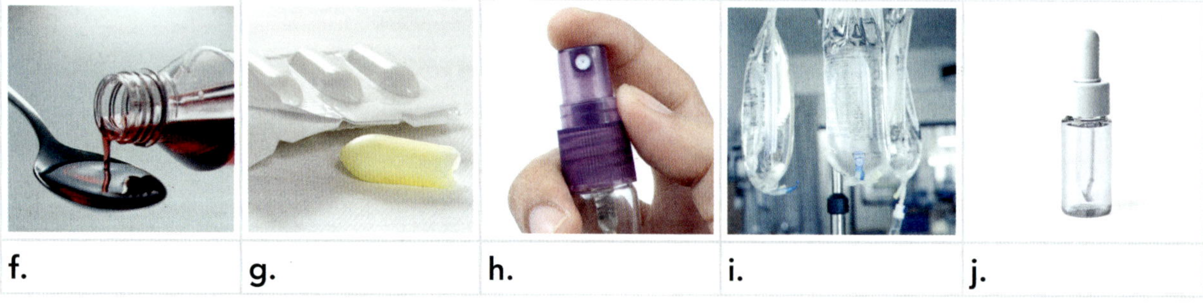

f.	**g.**	**h.**	**i.**	**j.**

NB: We can use the word *pill* to mean *tablet* or *capsule*, but '*the pill*' generally refers to oral contraception.

3 Match the routes of administration in the left column to the correct description in the right.

Route		Description	
a	inhalation → 5	1	under the tongue
b	instillation	2	into the eye or ear
c	intravenous → 8	3	through the skin
d	sublingual	4	into the rectum
e	rectal	5	into the lungs
f	topical	6	into the vagina
g	transdermal	7	by mouth
h	vaginal	8	through the vein
i	oral	9	through the nose
j	nasal	10	onto the skin

4 Now match the routes to the correct form of medication in 2.

Route		Medication form
a	inhalation	*inhaler*
b	instillation	
c	intravenous	*injection*
d	sublingual	
e	rectal	
f	topical	
g	transdermal	
h	vaginal	
i	oral	
j	nasal	

5 5.1 **A MAR (Medical Administration Records) chart is a record of medication administered to a service user. Read these MAR charts and complete these carer's instructions for their service user. Finally, listen to the audio and check your answers.**

a Take ______________________________

Name	Mina Patel	DOB	18/9/1945							
Allergies	None recorded	Doctor	Dr S. Singh							
Address	The Pines Nursing Home									
Start date	10/11/14	Period		Start day						
	Commencing date	Week 1								
		16	17	18	19	20	21	22	23	24
MEDICATION	Hours/Dose	1	2	3	4	5	6	7	1	2
Take 1 2 X a day Naproxen tablets BP 500 mg	Morn (080:00)	PF	PF	PF	D	PF				
	Noon (12:00)									
	Tea (17:00)	PF	PF	B	D	PF				
	Bed (21:00)									
Received		Quant		by		returned		quant		by

b Take ______________________________

Name	Peter Jones	DOB	20/5/1965							
Allergies	None recorded	Doctor	Dr S Singh							
Address	13 Oxford St. University									
Start date	1/11/11	Period		Start day						
	Commencing date	Week 1								
		16	17	18	19	20	21	22	23	24
MEDICATION	Hours/Dose	1	2	3	4	5	6	7	1	2
1 x 20 mg Atorvastatin Tablet Daily Morning.	Morn (080:00)	PF	PF	PF	D	PF	PF			
	Noon (12:00)									
	Tea (17:00)									
	Bed (21:00)									
Received		Quant		by		returned		quant		by

c ______________________________

Name	Irene Matthews	DOB	7/4/1930
Allergies	None recorded	Doctor	Dr S Singh
Address	2 Featherstone, Oldham, Lancs		
Start date	10/6/13	Period	Start day

	Commencing date	Week 1								
		16	17	18	19	20	21	22	23	24
MEDICATION	Hours/Dose	1	2	3	4	5	6	7	1	2
2 X Metformin 500 mg tablets twice daily just after food	Morn (080:00)	PF	PF	PF	D	PF	PF			
	Noon (12:00)									
	Tea (17:00)	PF	PF	B	D	PF	PF			
	Bed (21:00)									

Received		Quant		by		returned		quant		by

6 Write instructions for service users for these prescriptions.

a 2 x 250mg tablets 8 hourly if required:
Take two 250mg tablets every eight hours if you need to.

b 15ml x 2/day:

c 1 drop/3 x day:

d 1mg tablets – 1 dose/alternate days / 6 pm:

7 5.2 Listen to conversations with four service users and complete the table.

Service user	Medication	Uses	Form	Dose
a Derek	Codeine	*pain killer*	tablet	1 x ____mg up to 4 hourly
b Sylvie	Amoxil	____________	tablet	2 x 250mg ________
c Mrs Smith	Lactulose	____________	syrup	____ml, twice daily
d Mr Dawson	Azopt	*glaucoma*	______	____ drop per eye, ________

8 Re-order the words in the sentences below and practise explaining to a service user the difference between tablets and capsules.

a under the tongue / some tablets / dissolve / You can /

b However, / the little pills inside slowly / swallow capsules / you must / to release / whole

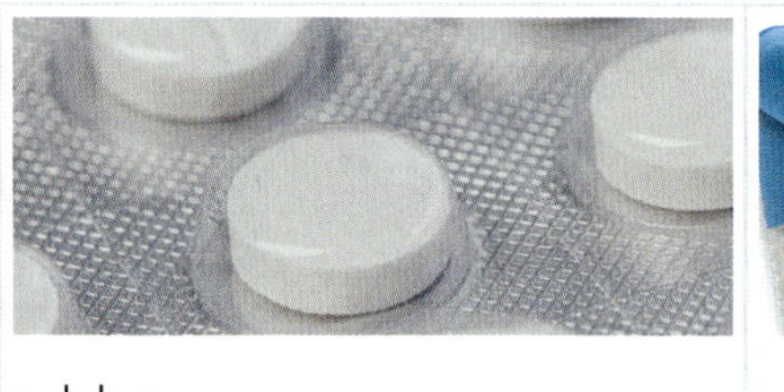
tablets

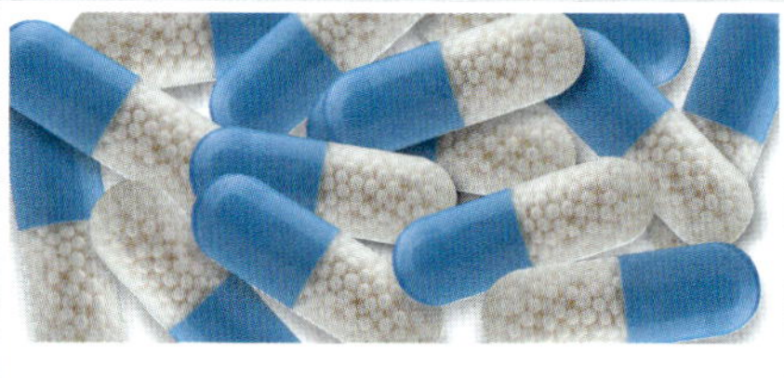
capsule

Administering medication

1 🔊 5.3 **We met Martha McDonald in Unit 3. Listen to Part 1 of the conversation with her carer, Josie. Underline the correct information in *italics* to complete the statements.**

a Josie is administering Martha's *morning / evening* medication.

b Martha uses a *monitored dosage pack / monitored package* to help check her medication.

c Josie is concerned about the correct *medication / dose*.

d The GP has changed the dose because Martha *experiences more pain / feels sick* in the morning.

2 Look at the stages for administering medication below. Number them in the correct order (1–8). Then go online to check.

		Stage
a	Update MAR chart.	*8*
b	Check if the service user is experiencing any pain.	
c	Put medication into the service user's hand and help them to take medication.	
d	Cross-check 'Seven Rights of Medication' with the service user and MAR chart.	
e	Ask for the service user's consent to administer medication.	*1*
f	Make sure the service user has taken the medication, and offer more water if necessary.	

g Check the service user has eaten, if necessary, and provide water.

h Put on personal protective equipment (PPE). *2*

3 🔊 5.3 **Listen again. Tick (✓) stages 1–3 as Martha's carer, Josie, carries them out.**

Stage 1 Stage 2 Stage 3

4 What do the underlined expressions mean? Use a dictionary to help you if necessary.

a You need to take them on a full stomach.

b I felt a bit queasy the other day.

c It wore off after an hour or so.

5 🔊 5.3 **Now listen to Part 2. Tick (✓) stages 4–8 from 2 as you hear them.**

Stage 4 Stage 5 Stage 6 Stage 7 Stage 8

6 🔊 5.3 **Re-order the words to form Josie's sentences. Listen to the whole dialogue and check your answers.**

a your morning / Are you / medication? / ready for *e*
eg *Are you ready for your morning medication?*

b eaten / Have / your breakfast? / you

c this morning? / How / your pain / is

d swallowed / Have / them? / you

e my / just / Let me / put / gloves on

f your MAR chart / just check this / Let me / with

g your water / are / your tablets / Here / and

h MAR chart / Now / sign / your / let me

7 Write the correct stage from 2 on p70 (a–h) next to Josie's sentences in 6.

REMEMBER!

Duty of care doesn't stop at simply administering medication. You must monitor and record (in the MAR chart) any adverse (bad) reactions or side effects to the medication you administer.

Grammar focus: Modals (*may/might*)

1 Read how we use *may* and *might* to talk about actions that are possible but not definite.

Use *may* or *might* + infinitive to talk about actions that are possible now or in the future.	*You* ***may/might*** *feel a little dizzy.* *The tablets* ***may/might*** *make you feel sick.*

2 Label the pictures with the correct side effect.

breathing difficulties	headache	rash	shaking	~~swelling~~	weight gain

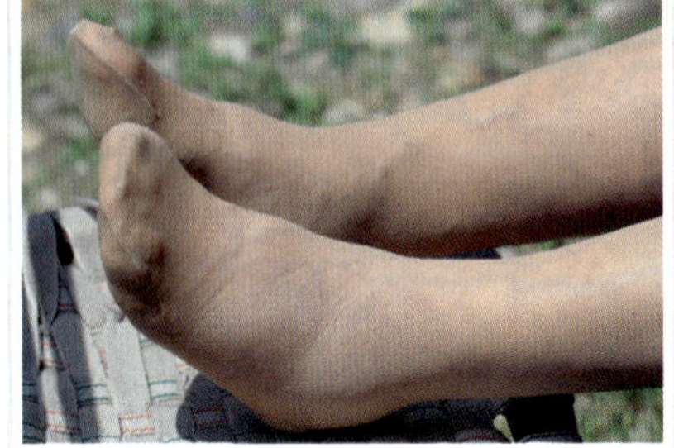

a *swelling*

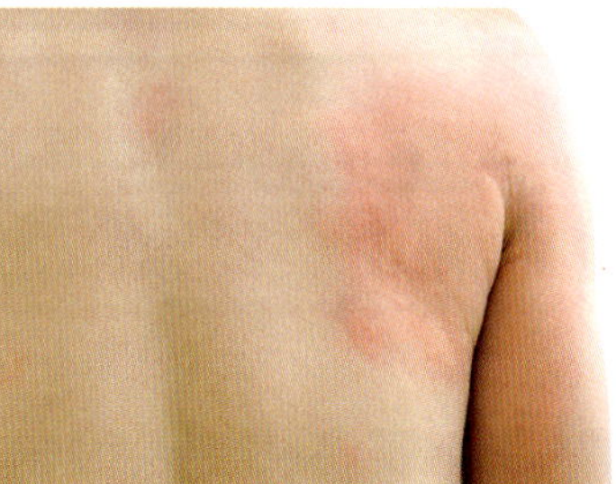

b ___________

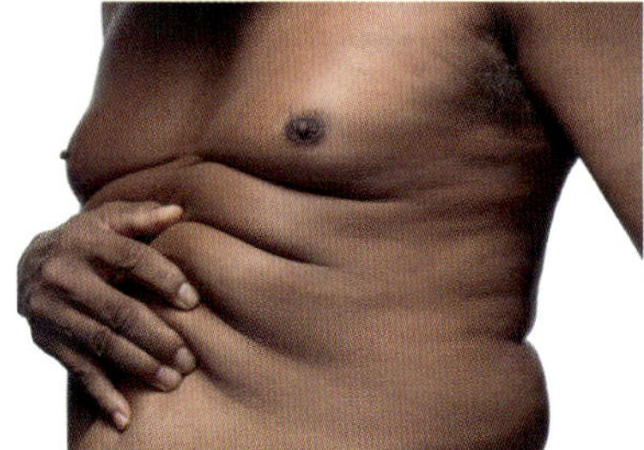

c ___________

d ___________

e ___________

f ___________

3 Think of two or three more possible side effects of medication? You may want to use a dictionary.

eg *nausea*

4 🔊 5.4 **Codeine is often used for pain relief. Add vowels to form the common side effects of codeine. Then listen and repeat what you hear.**

a Nausea, v__m__ting (or sickness) and c__nst__pati__n

b C__nf__sion, dr__wsin__ss, headache and d__zz__ness

c Dry m__uth, sw__at__ng and f__ci__l flushing

5 Complete the sentences below using *may/might* to inform service users about side effects.

a According to the leaflet / you / get / constipation
eg *According to the leaflet you may/might get constipation.*

b These tablets / cause / drowsiness

c They / make you / feel / sick

d You / suffer / nausea and vomiting

e You / experience / abdominal pains

f You / notice / some sweating

6 Here are some more side effects of codeine. Match them to the correct explanation.

Side effect	Explanation for a service user
a bradycardia → 5	1 (*be*) unable to empty your bladder
b hypotension	2 (*experience / notice*) a fast heart rate
c pruritus	3 (*experience / have / suffer*) breathing difficulties
d respiratory depression	4 (*make you*) itch
e tachycardia	5 (*experience / notice*) a slow heart rate
f urinary retention	6 (*experience / notice*) low blood pressure

7 Practise explaining the side effects of codeine to a service user. Use the verbs in brackets in 6.

eg *You may experience a slow heart rate. You might notice a slow heart rate.*

Medical focus: Stroke

1 Answer these questions about this common health issue.

a Roughly what percentage of people in the UK do you think die following a stroke?

b Which service users do you think are more likely to suffer from strokes?

c What causes a stroke?

2 5.5 **Before you listen, match the medical terms on the left to the descriptions. Then listen and repeat the terms as you hear them.**

Medical term		Descriptions	
a	artery	1	fatty deposit
b	atrial fibrillation	2	high blood pressure
c	hypertension	3	difficulty swallowing
d	ischemia	4	inability to move
e	plaque	5	irregular heart beat
f	dysphagia	6	major blood vessel
g	paralysis	7	severely reduced blood flow

3 **Read the text below and check your answers to the questions in 1** **(p73).**

Stroke

In the UK, not only are strokes the third largest cause of death, but resulting brain injuries are also a major reason for disability in adults. Those most at risk include people of South Asian, African or Caribbean origin who have a predisposition to hypertension, which can lead to strokes. Others at risk are those with high cholesterol, atrial fibrillation or diabetes, as well as people who are overweight or who smoke.

Causes: Around 85% of strokes are ischemic strokes, caused by arteries connecting to the brain narrowing or becoming blocked. Plaque cause blood clots to form within the arteries, which results in ischemia. The brain is then deprived of oxygen and nutrients, which stops it functioning normally.

4 **Before you read the next part of the text, write down three or four symptoms of a stroke. Then read and check your answers.**
eg *dizziness*

Symptoms:

Somebody suspected of suffering a stroke may have weakness or numbness in one arm; their speech may appear slurred and their face may have dropped on one side. Other symptoms include complete paralysis of one side of the body, sudden loss or blurring of vision, dizziness, confusion, communication problems such as dysphasia, problems with balance and co-ordination, dysphagia, a sudden and very severe headache or loss of consciousness.

5 **Cover the text you've just read and practise describing an ischemic stroke to a service user. Avoid using medical terms where possible.**

6 **Go online and find out about haemorrhagic strokes and transient ischemic attacks (TIAs) or mini-strokes.**

Consider:

- Causes
- Symptoms
- Prevention (F.A.S.T.)

Asking about pain

1 **Read the following quotation. What does Anita want to remind carers?**

'If you alleviate [ease] the pain, you actually lift people's mood and make them feel better.'

(*Anita Astle, Managing Director, Wren Hall Nursing Home: www.scie.org.uk*)

Match these common pain expressions on the left to the correct definition.

	Pain expression		Definition
a	It aches. / It's aching. → 3	1	It is slightly painful when touched.
b	It hurts. / It's painful.	2	The pain of open wounds, ulcers or the throat.
c	It's itchy. / It itches. / It's itching.	3	A dull continuous pain.
d	It's sore.	4	General description for mild or moderate pain.
e	It's tender.	5	A feeling on the skin that makes you want to scratch.

3 5.6 **Listen and match the pain expressions (1–4) to the correct service user.**

1 It's a bit tender.

2 It doesn't hurt, but it's very itchy.

3 It's very painful.

4 It really aches.

a Alice

b Mr Khan

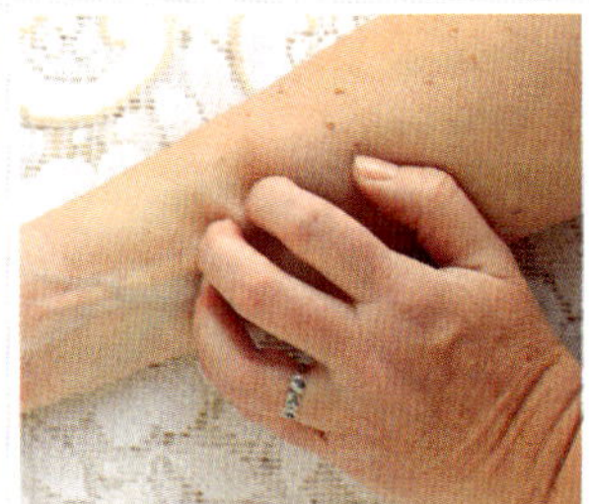

c Anne

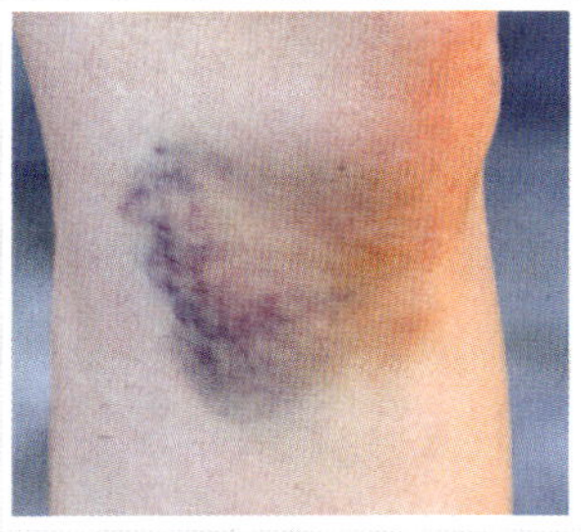

d Howard

4 🔊 5.6 **Complete the carers' questions. Then listen to the audio and check your answers.**

a	*How* are you feeling this morning?	d	______ you tell me where the pain is?
b	______ does it hurt?	e	______ anything bothering you?
c	______ you in any pain?	f	______ you point to where it hurts?

5 Everyone feels pain differently. Re-order the words for asking about pain with reference to the pain assessment tool (pain scale).

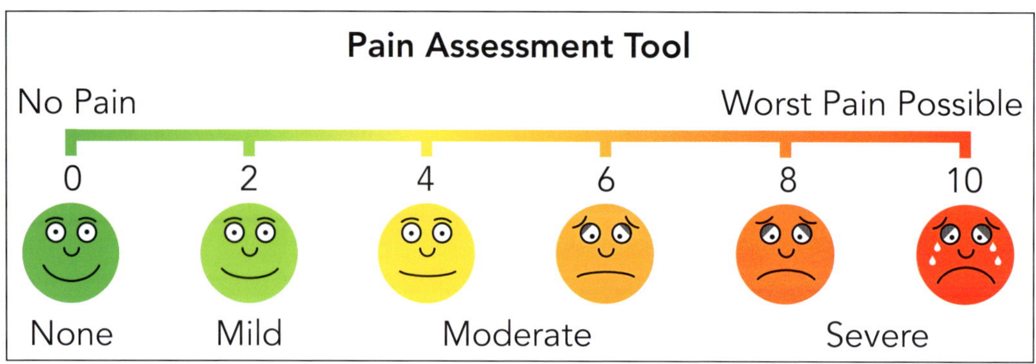

a is it / 0 to 10? / on a scale of / How painful

b the worst pain possible / no pain / 0 is / 10 is / and

6 Practise asking the service users in 3 about their pain. Use the questions from 4 and 5.

7 Some service users can't talk about their pain. Read these comments from carers. Then add vowels (*a, e, i, o, u*) to complete questions for their service users.

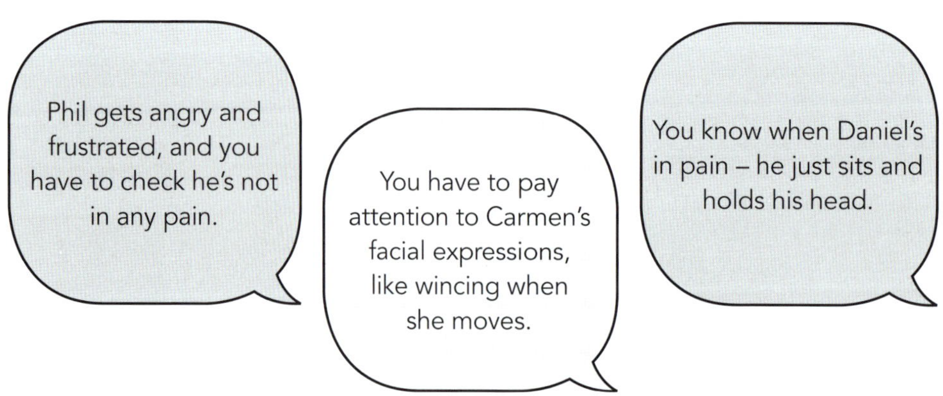

a C_n y_u sh_w m_ _n th_ p_in sca_l_?

b P_int t_ th_ p_ct_re _n th_ pa_in sc_l_ f_r m_.

8 Practise asking the service users in 7 about their pain. You may want to begin like this:

a Phil, I see you're rubbing your shoulder ...

b I noticed you winced when you moved, Carmen, ...

c You look tired, Daniel, …

9 Some service users find it difficult to take their medication. Read the comments below and match the piece(s) of advice (1–6) to the correct service user.

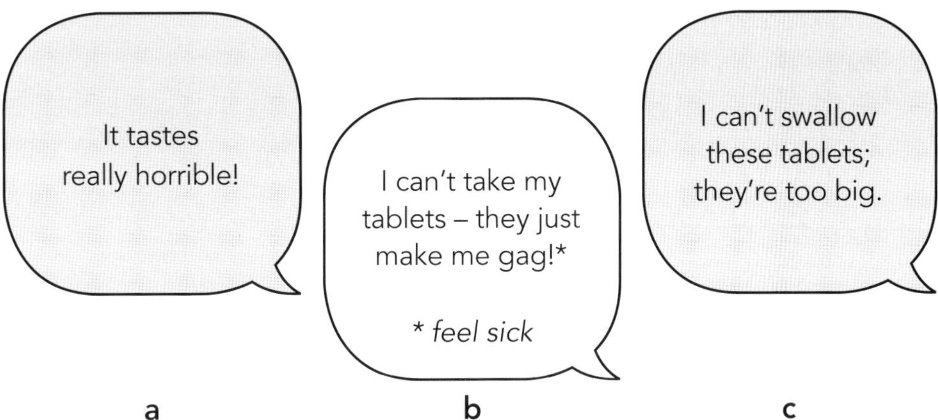

1 Place the pill in the centre of your tongue (or lengthways if the pill is oval).

2 Take a sip of water immediately and throw your head back to wash the pill down.

3 Swallow the tablet together with a piece of bread.

4 Take a deep breath to help stop your gag reflex.

5 Try chewing some food before placing the pill in your mouth. Then swallow both together.

6 Put your chin on your chest when you swallow to help close your windpipe.

10 Practise giving the service users in 9 advice for taking their medication. You may want to use these expressions:

Why don't you … Try … You could … You might want to …

Study skills (2): Recording and learning new vocabulary

1 Read this text from a reference book for social care students. Then tick (✓) the sentence below (a–d) that is correct for you.

Monitored Dosage System (MDS)

There are a variety of medical devices to enable people to take their medicines. The pharmacist may dispense medicine in bottles and boxes or in a Monitored Dosage System (MDS).

Also known as a dosette box, an MDS is usually used for solid oral dose medicines eg tablets and capsules, and a system that dispenses unit doses of liquids also now exists. Other formulations such as inhalers, eye drops, creams and ointments and effervescent tablets cannot be dispensed by an MDS. This results in two different systems of medicine administration being used in the home, which may cause problems.

It is vital that good practice prevails and the MAR chart is always referred to before the administration to ensure that all the medicines prescribed are given to the correct person, regardless of how they are dispensed.

Source: Adapted from Good Practice Guidance E – Monitored Dosage Systems in Care Homes, NHS (2015)

a I understood the whole text.

b I didn't understand every word, but I understood the main points of the text.

c I understood some of the main points.

d I didn't understand anything.

2 Try reading the text again using techniques for reading from Unit 3 (see pp48 & 49).

3 What are the advantages of using a monolingual dictionary? Add two or three more examples. Go online to check your answers.

- Find out about common collocations (a group of words that are usually used together).
- Check the pronunciation.
- Learn the part of speech. For example, is it a noun, adjective or verb?

4 Look at the definition of 'medication' and find one example of each of the points in 3.

> **medication**
>
> noun [mass noun]
>
> a drug or other form of medicine that is used to treat or prevent disease: he was given medication for pain | certain medications can cause dizziness.
>
> treatment using drugs: chronic gastrointestinal symptoms may require prolonged medication.

5 Read this advice from other social carers to help you understand new vocabulary.

Use your own knowledge of English and the subject to guess the meaning.

Look at the words around the new word to help guess the meaning.

Use your knowledge of other foreign languages (eg French) to help guess the meaning.

Use visual clues eg photos, to help you understand the meaning.

6 Look at these extracts from the text in 1 on p78. Which piece(s) of advice would *you* follow from 5 to help you understand the underlined words?

a There are a variety of medical devices to enable people to take their medicines.

b … an MDS is usually used for solid oral dose medicines eg tablets and capsules …

c Other formulations such as inhalers, eye drops, creams and ointments …

d It is vital that good practice prevails …

7 Re-order these words to form tips for recording and learning new vocabulary.

a remember them / as you write them / to help you /pronounce and / Say words aloud /

b sentence / in a meaningful / new word / Write the

c around your study area / on post-it notes / Write new words / and stick them

d until you are confident /you know the words / every two days and / every three days / Then test yourself

e or waiting for the train/ test yourself while / Write new words / in a notebook and / you are on the bus

8 Choose one of Units 6–10. Use tips from 7 to record and learn 10 new words about your chosen unit.

Unit 6

Health and safety

Target areas

• Assessing and reassuring a service user • Calling the emergency services • Modals for expressing obligation: *must, have to, should* • Understanding a risk assessment • Reporting an incident • Medical focus: Epilepsy • Report writing (3) • Past tense review

In their shoes

1 Label these causes of possible accidents in the home. Use the words in the boxes.

accidental poisoning	burns and scalds	electrocution
injuries from operating machinery	sharps injury	~~trips and falls~~

a *trips and falls*

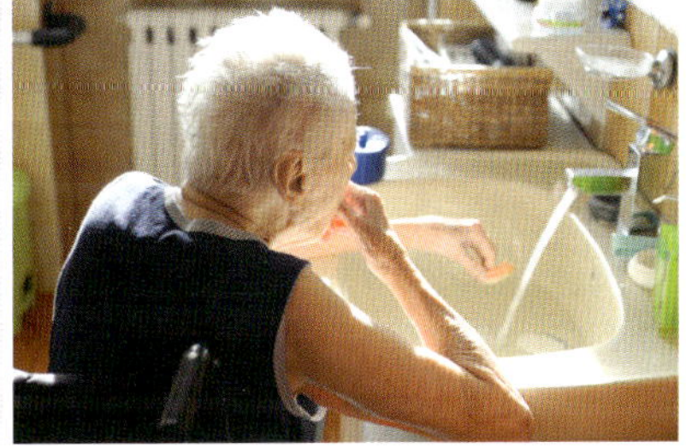

b ___________

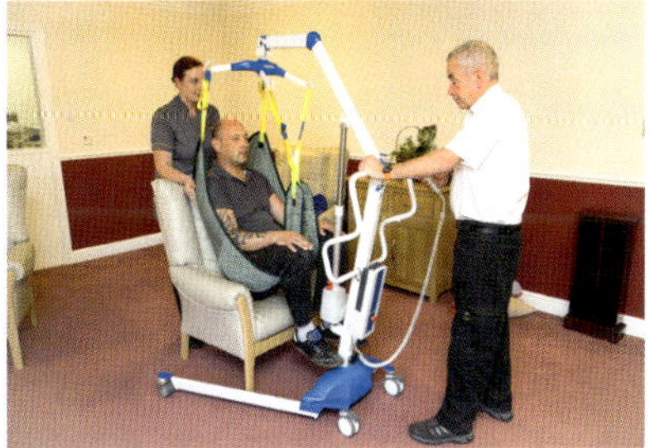

c ___________

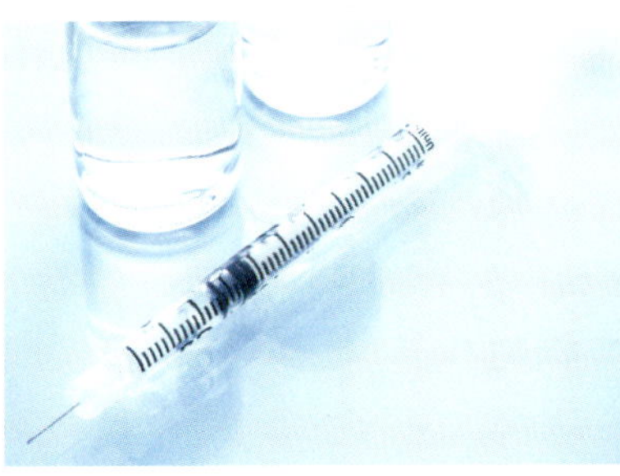

d ___________

e ___________

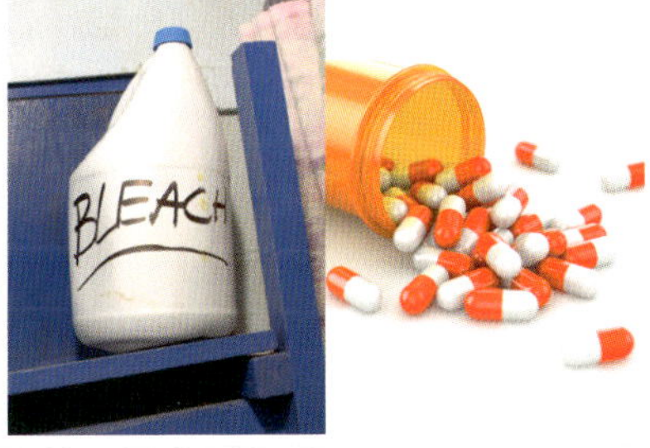

f ___________

2 Think about your own home. Write down three or four possible dangers:

a in your kitchen **b** in your bathroom **c** in your garden

3 A service user might become ill suddenly. Write three or four examples of sudden illness that a carer might have to respond to.

eg *diabetic coma*

Assessing and reassuring a service user

1 Read the information about Phyllis. What are common risk factors for service users like Phyllis?

eg *limited mobility*

Phyllis Jones (81) lives in her own two-storey house. Phyllis is short-sighted and has arthritis, which limits the use of her hands. She therefore needs support with tasks that require fine motor skills. She needs assistance twice a day to help her with meal preparation and light housework. Her carer, Rosie, arrives one day to find Phyllis lying at the bottom of her stairs.

2 What should Rosie do? Write *T* (true) or *F* (false) for each statement.

a	Remain calm and send for help.	*T*
b	Observe Phyllis, listen and try to find out what happened.	
c	Move Phyllis to a warm place, if possible.	
d	Reassure Phyllis.	
e	Stay with Phyllis until help arrives, noting any changes in her condition.	
f	Ask her manager to complete an incident report and inform Phyllis's family members.	

3 Correct any false statements in 2.

4 6.1 **Listen to Rosie and Phyllis and tick (✓) the steps in 2 as you hear them.**

a ☐ b ☐ c ☐ d ☐ e ☐ f ☐

5 🔊 6.1 **Read the questions, then listen again and choose the correct answer for each one.**

a	What was the probable cause of the accident?		
	1 ill-fitting footwear	**2** confusion	**3** arthritis
b	Where does Phyllis feel pain?		
	1 Her left shoulder hurts	**2** Her right leg and shoulder hurt	**3** Her right leg is bruised
c	What does Rosie do to make Phyllis more comfortable?		
	1 Covers her with a blanket	**2** Moves her to the living room	**3** Puts her coat on
d	What is Rosie going to do about her work schedule?		
	1 Call her next client	**2** Ask another carer to attend to her next client	**3** Inform her manager of the situation

6 Assess (A) means to understand the situation. Reassure (R) means to stop someone from worrying. Look at Rosie's expressions and write *A* or *R* next to each one.

a	Can you tell me what happened?	*A*	d	How are you feeling, not too cold?	
b	Try to stay calm.		e	I need to be sure you haven't broken anything.	
c	I'll stay here until the ambulance comes.		f	Does it hurt anywhere?	

7 🔊 6.2 **Listen and complete more reassuring expressions.**

a I'm ____________ you.

b ____________ worry.

c You're ____________. Take some ____________.

d Try ____________. There's a lot of blood, but I think it ____________.

e You must ____________. We're trying everything to make things ____________.

f The ambulance ____________.

8 🔊 6.2 **Listen again and repeat what you hear.**

9 Record your voice until you are happy that you sound reassuring.

NB: To sound reassuring, lower the tone of your voice and speak a little slower than normal.

Calling the emergency services

1 How confident are you on the telephone in English? Put a cross (X) on the continuum.

I'm not confident using the telephone in an emergency.	←——————→	I feel very confident using the telephone in an emergency.

2 What makes it difficult for you to communicate by telephone in English?

eg *I find it difficult when the other speaker has a strong accent.*

3 🔊 6.3 **Rosie calls 999. Listen and underline the words in *italics* to complete the statements.**

a Rosie asks to speak to the *ambulance / fire* service.

b Rosie arrived and found Phyllis *lying at the bottom of the stairs / was still in bed.*

c The ambulance will arrive in *20 minutes / 30 minutes.*

d The operator advises Rosie to *make sure Phyllis is warm / make Phyllis a cup of tea.*

4 🔊 6.3 **Match the two halves to form the operator's questions. Then listen and check your answers.**

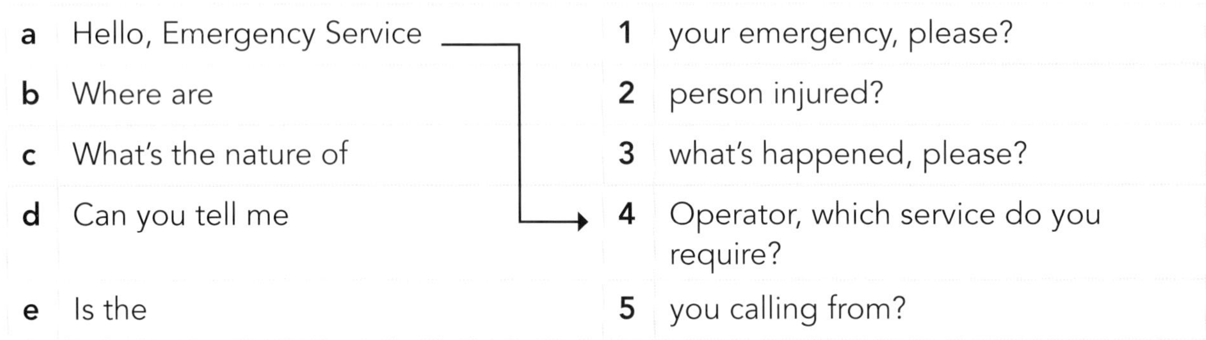

a	Hello, Emergency Service → 4	1	your emergency, please?
b	Where are	2	person injured?
c	What's the nature of	3	what's happened, please?
d	Can you tell me	4	Operator, which service do you require?
e	Is the	5	you calling from?

5 🔊 6.4 **Use the transcript online and practise calling the emergency services. Take the role of Rosie.**

6 Add vowels (*a, e, i, o, u*) to complete these useful telephone expressions.

a I c_n't he_r y_u v_ry w_ll.

b It's a r_ally b_d l_ne.

c My b_tt_ry's r_nning l_w.

d I d_dn't c_tch wh_t y_u sa_d.

e C_n yo_ r_pe_t th_t, ple_s_?

f C_n y_u sp_ak m_re sl_wly, ple_s_?

7 Practise saying the expressions in 6. We usually add *'(I'm) sorry …'* or *'I'm afraid …'* before each expression to sound more polite.

8 Read the notes of three incidents which have occurred in the home. Practise calling the emergency services. What information do you need to give the operator?

a Peter Bennett (63), feeling dazed, taken analgesics (pain killers), scalded in shower

b Maggie Widdowson (75), visually impaired, taken wrong dose

c Winston Taylor (73), early onset dementia, electrocuted trying to fix iron

Grammar focus: Modals (*must, have to, should*)

1 Read how to use modals *must*, *have to* and *should*.

Use *must* or *have to* + infinitive to express obligation. Use *should* + infinitive to make a strong recommendation or give advice. Use *have to*, NOT *must*, for questions. Use *must*, NOT *have to* to express negative obligation.	▶ *You **must** be at work at 9.00.* ▶ *You **have to** wear an apron at all times.* ▶ *You **should** put the medication out of the reach of your grandchildren.* ▶ *Do I **have to** put on my gloves?* ▶ *You **mustn't** throw needles in the bin.*
NB: *You don't have to wear an apron = There's no obligation to wear an apron.*	

2 Label the pictures of hazardous waste with the words in the boxes.

cleaning materials	clinical waste	contaminated bed linen	disinfectants	medication

a

b

c

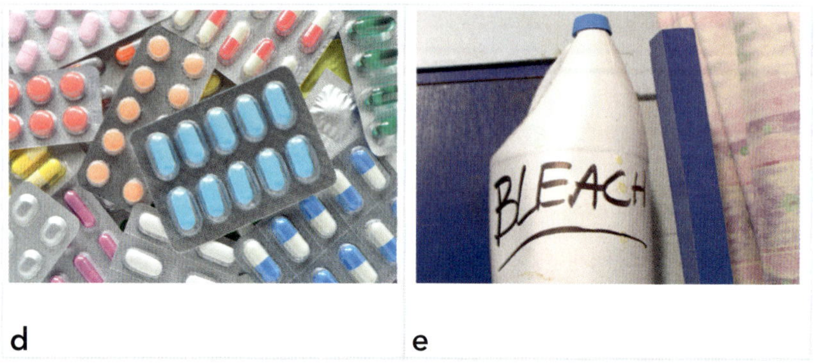

d

e

3 Use the verbs in brackets and the correct modal from 1 (p85) to complete the information.

a You <u>*don't have to put*</u> the bed linen in a separate bag, but it's a good idea. *(put)*

b You ______________ the instructions for administering her medication. *(follow)*

c For your own safety you ______only ________ products that are in their original containers. *(use)*

d You ______________ cleaning products and disinfectants out of the reach of vulnerable adults. *(keep)*

e You ______________ service users not to pour cleaning fluids into unmarked bottles. *(advise)*

4 🔊 6.5 A care home manager is training Rachel, a new carer. Complete the expressions below with modals from 1 (p85). Listen and check your answers.

Manager: You **(a)** <u>*must be*</u> very careful with clinical waste. So anything that's contaminated – dressings, bandages, anything you've used to clean the service user – you have to put all of those in the yellow clinical waste bags.

Rachel: What about our aprons and gloves? Do we **(b)** ________ put those in there too?

Manager: Yes, you do. Disposable items used for cleaning the spills, such as paper towels and gloves, **(c)** ________ also be disposed of as clinical waste. And sharps, do you know what you **(d)** ________ do with sharps?

Rachel: I guess we **(e)** ________ put those in the sharps box, right?

Manager: Right. You **(f)** ________ follow the correct procedure for the care home you're working at. Now if you're doing domiciliary work, then you **(g)** ________ really send the sharps box back to the user's pharmacy or surgery.

Rachel: Oh, OK, I didn't know I had to do that.

Manager: And don't forget, body fluids such as blood, urine, vomit and faeces **(h)** ________ cleaned up immediately.

Rachel: OK, I think I understand.

Manager: You **(i)** ________ always check with your manager if you're not sure.

REMEMBER!

Read the COSHH (Control of Substances Hazardous to Health) file in your place of work for information about the substances you are asked to use. *http://www.hse.gov.uk/coshh/basics/substance.htm*

Understanding a risk assessment

1 Read the quotation. Do you agree or disagree?

'Risk assessments are not about restricting what people do, they are about making sure that it is done safely.'

(Y Nolan, Health and Social Care Level 2, Heinemann 2011)

2 Skim the risk assessment for Phyllis Jones overleaf and complete the notes that follow.

NB. ignore the underlined words until activity 3.

Risk Assessment

SunnyView CARE

Name: Phyllis Jones

Person completing the risk assessment: Gruff Jones (Social Worker)

Body build: Small–medium

Problems: Not using the stairs safely in the morning before staff arrive.

Handling constraints: Phyllis is short-sighted and has arthritis, and this can result in her being particularly vulnerable when using the stairs in the morning. This is exacerbated by the fact that she often forgets to put her glasses on when getting up, as she tends to be a little confused in the mornings and wobbly on her feet. All of which can severely impact on her ability to use the stairs first thing in the morning.

Tasks: Using the stairs safely.

Methods to be used: Staff should encourage Phyllis to stay upstairs until they arrive in the morning. Once staff arrive, they should ensure that she is fully awake, wearing her glasses and able to negotiate the stairs safely without the risk of falling. Phyllis should be encouraged to take a glass of water to bed with her and any other items that she needs to negate the need for her to come downstairs during the night.

Any remaining problems: Staff should remind Phyllis to try to stay upstairs at night unless there is an emergency and she needs to vacate the house via the stairs.

Date: 27/07/2016

Assessor: Gruff Jones

Review Date: 27/01/2017

Who? Phyllis Jones

What? Service user might ________________

Why? Service user short sighted / has ___________ / gets _________ + forgets to put on ___________

When? _____________ before the carers arrive

How? Discourage service user from _____________ before carers arrive.

Advise her to_______ / _________________ (glass water etc.)

Only take stairs _______________

3 Match the <u>underlined</u> words or expressions in 2 to the correct definition.

	Definition	Word / expression
a	Adjective used to describe someone who needs special care or support	*vulnerable*
b	To make something worse	
c	To have a strong effect on something	
d	To leave	
e	To invalidate or cancel	

4 How does the risk assessment in 2 try to respond to the quotation in 1?

5 Practise giving advice to Phyllis. Use the information in the risk assessment or any of your own ideas. You may want to use modals (*should, have to, must*) or these expressions:

- *It's a good idea to …*
- *It's really important that you …*
- *It's better to … / It's better not to … / It's not a good idea to …*

Reporting an incident

1 You were introduced to service users Marina Staples and Martin Cropper in Unit 4. What do you remember about them?

Marina

Martin

eg *Marina lives in a residential care home. Martin has muscular dystrophy.*

2 🔊 6.6 **Carers Rosie and Amit are reporting incidents experienced by Marina and Martin. Listen and <u>underline</u> the correct incident for each service user.**

a *Marina:* fall / scalding / wrong dosage

b *Martin:* bruising / swelling / fainting

3 🔊 6.6 **Listen again and complete the statements about each incident.**

a Marina was trying to *<u>reach the dining room</u>* from ______________ when she suddenly felt faint.

b The GP said Marina had a problem with ______________.

c Duty Manager Sanja asked Rosie to ______________.

d Martin is upset about ______________.

e Duty Manager Patrick asked Amit to ______________.

f Amit should always ______________ if he's __________ about a service user.

4 Write *C* (Carer) or *M* (manager) for each statement in [6.6].

a	How can I help?	*M*
b	I need to report an incident	
c	I called the GP out.	
d	What was the GP's assessment?	
e	Can you fill in an Accident Form, please?	
f	Thanks for informing me.	
g	What should I do?	
h	Thanks for calling. You did the right thing.	
i	If in doubt, always seek medical assistance.	

5 Rosie is reporting Phyllis's incident to her manager, John. Look at the expressions from 4 and adapt them to complete the conversation.

Rosie: Hi, John, it's Rosie.

John: Hello, Rosie **(a)** ________________?

Rosie: **(b)** ________________ at Phyllis's home today.

John: Oh dear, is everything OK?

Rosie: Yes, Phyllis is fine now, but when I arrived she had fallen down the stairs.

John: Did you call **(c)** ________________?

Rosie: No, I had to call the emergency services. She has some bruising on her right shoulder and left thigh. Apart from being a little shaken, she's OK. Her daughter is with her now.

John: And what was the ambulance crew's **(d)** ________________?

Rosie: They've assessed her as being OK.

John: Oh that's good. **(e)** ________________ and drop it in to me as soon as you can?

Rosie: Yes, that's fine, John, I'll do that.

John: **(f)** ________________ of the incident. Have a good day.

6 6.7 **Listen and practise reporting the incident involving Phyllis Jones to the manager. Take the role of Rosie.**

Medical focus: Epilepsy

1 Read these statistics and think about the questions below.

- More than three million people in the US live with epilepsy.
- Around 1 in 100 people experience some form of epilepsy in the UK.
- There are over 40 types of epilepsy.

a Do the statistics surprise you? Why (not)?

b What is your experience of epilepsy?

c What happens during an epileptic seizure?

2 **As you read the information about epilepsy, complete the text with the expressions in the boxes.**

those over 65	drug and alcohol abuse	seizures or 'fits'	involuntary responses in the body
bowel and bladder	lose consciousness	'trance-like' state	

Living with epilepsy

What causes epilepsy?

Although the cause is not always possible to identify, epilepsy is usually diagnosed in children and **(a)** *those over 65*. The condition can be caused by a severe head injury, stroke or brain tumour, as well as **(b)** __________.

What happens?

Tonic-clonic seizures, referred to as **(c)** __________ are most commonly associated with epilepsy and can last a few minutes, sometimes longer. Seizures occur when the brain receives a burst of abnormal electrical signals. This temporarily interrupts the normal brain function and causes **(d)** __________. During a seizure people might **(e)** __________, suffer convulsions and even lose **(f)** __________ control. However, not everyone experiences seizures; some may simply go into a **(g)** __________ for a few seconds.

3 Check your answer to 1c.

4 6.8 **Listen to a trainer explaining the correct procedure during a seizure. Tick (✓) the correct instruction. Listen again and check your answers.**

		Must	Must not
a	Stop the service user from hurting themselves.	✓	
b	Move the service user to a safe warm place.		
c	Stop the service user from swallowing their tongue using your fingers.		
d	Turn the service user on their side into the recovery position.		
e	Talk to the service user and try to reassure them.		
f	If the service user experiences breathing difficulties, call 999.		

5 Read the transcript online and find words and expressions the trainer uses that mean the same as these.

a support: *cushion*

b hold them down: __________

c shaking/fitting: __________

d come round: __________

e breathing difficulties: __________

6 Practise explaining to a new carer how to take care of a service user during a seizure. Use any of the expressions in 5 and modals *must*, *have to* and *should*.

eg *You must try to stop the service user from hurting themselves.*

7 Go online and find out about:

- non-epileptic seizures
- the recovery position
- treating epilepsy

Report writing (3)

1 We can use conjunctions, eg *when* and *while*, to talk about two actions happening at the same time. Read the Daily Care Report for Phyllis Jones. Underline the conjunctions that indicate time.

Daily Care Report SunnyView CARE

Date am/pm	Observations *(please include information such as personal care given, food eaten, general mood and state of service user etc.)*	Name of carer	Signature of carer
20.06.16	Phyllis was waiting for me at the window when I arrived this evening at 6.00. She was still a little shaken from her fall this morning but was putting on a brave face. We prepared her evening meal together – Phyllis asked for a cheese and tomato omelette and salad. Her younger daughter, Sandra, called round to see her while we were cooking. During the meal, I reminded Phyllis to wait for me to arrive in the mornings before getting out of bed. Phyllis ate most of her dinner. Evening medication given and signed for. As I was leaving, Phyllis's son called from Canada to check up on her. Phyllis was in a cheery mood when I left.	Rosie Turner	R.Turner

Grammar focus: Past tense review

2 Read how we use the past simple and past continuous tenses.

Use the **past simple** to talk/write about a finished action.	*eg I arrived at 1.30.*
Use the **past continuous** to talk/write about an action that was in progress when something else happened.	*eg Marina was sitting in the living room when I arrived.*
NB. We don't use the present continuous for verbs which describe states, such as *be, like, love.*	*eg Marina was in a good mood when I left. (Not: Marina was being in a good mood)*

3 Cover the report in 1. Use the verbs in brackets in the correct form to complete the statements.

a Phyllis <u>was waiting</u> for me at the window when I ________ this evening at 6.00. (*wait / arrive*)

b Her younger daughter, Sandra, ________ to see her while we ________. (*call round / cook*)

c During the meal, I ________ Phyllis to wait for me to arrive in the mornings before getting out of bed. (*remind*)

d As I ________, Phyllis's son ________ from Canada to check up on her. (*leave / phone*)

e Phyllis ________ in a cheery mood when I ________. (*be / leave*)

4 Use the verbs in the boxes in the correct form to complete report entries for service user Marjorie Wallis.

arrive	be	break	call	contact	fall
lie	manage	stumble	take	~~trip~~	

a Marjorie *<u>tripped</u>* and _____ while she _____ her dog for a walk in the park.

b During their walk, Marjorie _____ on a loose paving stone and _____ her right hip.

c While she _____ on the grass, Marjorie _____ to text her neighbour, who came to help her.

d Just as her neighbour _____ the emergency services, Marjorie's son, Denis, _____.

e While Marjorie _____ in hospital, the nurse _____ social services to arrange for post-discharge support.

Unit 7

Activities of Daily Living

Target areas

• Assisting with shopping • Encouraging independence • Using public transport • Visiting the GP • Reported speech • Medical focus: Angina • Study skills (4): Listening and note-taking

In their shoes

1 Look at the pictures. Write down three or four other 'activities of daily living' (ADLs).

a Shopping

b Using public transport

c Visiting the GP

2 Imagine you live alone and you break your leg. Write down three or four problems you would have carrying out the ADLs in 1.

eg *mobility*

3 Were these comments made by service users (SU) or carers (C)? Write *SU*, *C* or both (B).

a I've learnt it's important to do things with, not for, people. *C*

b I want to feel like I'm a human being.

c If I had the choice of living somewhere else, I would say no, I want to live here.

d Because I live a certain way, it doesn't mean it's the right way for them.

e If you haven't got someone to rely on, you've had it.

**4 What do you think about the comments in 3?
Do you agree or disagree? Why?**

**5 Read this extract from a reference book on social care.
Answer the questions that follow.**

> **The Importance of Independence**
>
> Developing and maintaining independence is important as it helps service users achieve their goals and feel in control. It also allows them to contribute to society, which has positive rewards. There are health benefits to independence; it even helps maintain a healthy heart! However, loss of independence can have a negative effect on a service user's mental state eg they might become isolated, stop participating in their usual activities, begin to neglect their homes etc. Service users might then begin to lose confidence in themselves. In addition, from a financial point of view, it is very expensive to employ care workers to carry out basic ADLs which service users may well be capable of doing themselves with a little assistance.

a What are the physical benefits of independence?

b How can a lack of independence affect a service user emotionally?

c What are the additional problems associated with lack of independence amongst service users?

Assisting with shopping

**1 Put the food items into the correct category.
Use a dictionary if necessary.**

Bakery items	Fresh food	Frozen foods	Store cupboard foods
			tin of sweetcorn

2 Think about a service user you know.
Add two or three items he or she would buy into each category.

3 Underline the odd one out in each list.
Use the correct label from the box for each category.

home entertainment	household	~~pets~~	toiletries

Items	Category
a cat food, *washing-up liquid*, dog biscuits, lead	*pets*
b conditioner, lipstick, bleach, flannel	
c washing powder, saucepan, bin liners, flour	
d DVD, *Your Health* magazine, headphones, towel	

4 Read about service user Jamila.

Jamila (19) has a mild learning disability. She is making up her weekly shopping list. Robert, her personal assistant, is helping her to do this.

5 🔊 7.1 **Listen and complete the weekly meal planner for Jamila.**

Mon	Tues	Wed	Thurs	Fri	Sat	Sun
Spaghetti bolognaise						

6 🔊 7.1 **Listen again and write out Jamila's shopping list.**

1 Match the words (a–f) to the correct definition (1–6).

Word		Definition	
a	credit	1	money charged for taking the bus/ train
b	fare	2	to pass a card through an electronic reader
c	stop	3	list of times when the bus departs
d	swipe	4	money available on a travel card to pay for bus/train
e	timetable	5	to add money to a travel card
f	top up	6	place where passengers can get on/ off the bus

2 Read more information about Jamila from the previous section. What problems do you think Jamila might have travelling independently by bus?

eg *Understanding the bus timetable*

Jamila is about to start a college course in catering. She wants to travel independently from her flat to the college. She is doing some travel training today with Robert.

3 7.2 **Robert checks that Jamila can use the bus. Listen to Part 1 and complete his questions.**

a Now, where's your __________?

b Can you remember which bus we __________?

c How often do we need to __________?

d And __________ top it up?

4 7.2 **Listen to Part 1 again and answer Robert's questions in 3.**

a *In her bag.* b __________ c __________ d __________

5 7.2 **Listen to Part 2 and complete the information.**

Robert reminds Jamila to …

a hold __________ before she gets on the bus.

b __________ as she gets on the bus.

c __________ so she knows where to get off.

d __________ as she gets off the bus.

6 7.2 **Match a–d with 1–4 to form Robert's reminders for Jamila. Listen and check your answers.**

a	Make sure you've got → 3	1	thank the driver.
b	Don't forget to swipe	2	sign at the front of the bus.
c	Make sure you watch the	3	your travel card in your hand ready.
d	Remember to	4	your travel card first.

7 7.3 **It's important to use a friendly tone. Listen and repeat the reminders in 6.**

Encouraging independence

1 Read about service user Matt Bartholomew. How can Samantha and Ann make sure Matt is as involved as possible in preparing his meals?

Matt Bartholomew (40) has Downs Syndrome and lives with four other men in a group home. He has a moderate learning disability which affects his ability to care for himself effectively. He requires support to manage his ADLs. While he is generally happy, sometimes Matt can become distressed and depressed, especially when his mum goes away and misses her regular visits. His mum is very important to him. Matt has two carers, Ann and Samantha, who assist him on alternate days and have different approaches to his care. Matt enjoys cooking, and he likes helping Ann and Samantha prepare meals.

Matt and his mum

2 Read the two conversations and answer the questions.

Conversation A

Samantha: Let me write the shopping list. I've not got much time this morning, so we need to do this quickly and then go and do the shopping. So you need meat for your stew, right?

Matt: Yes, meat, yes, that's good.

Samantha: So, that's beef and carrots. Do you want any other vegetables? Turnips, maybe?

Matt: Yes, OK.

Samantha: Good, so that's beef, carrots and turnips. Sounds good, doesn't it?

Matt: Yes, I think so.

Conversation B

Ann: Let's write the shopping list together. What do you need for your stew, Matt?

Matt: Meat.

Ann: That's right. What kind of meat do you normally use for your stew?

Matt: I don't know.

Ann: Do you want beef, chicken, pork …?

Matt: Beef is good.

Ann: OK, so you need beef and …?

Matt: Carrots.

Ann: Good, and what else do you need?

Matt: Peas.

Ann: Uh huh?

Matt: Erm, I don't know.

Ann: How about turnips?

Matt: No, no, I don't like turnips. Swede. Can I put swede in my stew?

Ann: Mmmmm, that sounds like a good idea. You're doing really well, Matt.

Matt: I think it's going to be very tasty.

- **a** What ingredients does Matt need in Conversation A? What does he need in Conversation B?
- **b** What do we learn about Samantha?
- **c** Which meal is Matt more likely to enjoy – A or B? Why?

3 Which carer – Samantha or Ann – encourages Matt to be more independent? How?

4 We can use different techniques to encourage independence. Add examples from the conversations in 2 (p100) to complete the table.

Technique	Example
Open questions (Questions that encourage the service user to give more information, not just *Yes/No*)	*Do you want any other vegetables?*
Giving suggestions	*Do you want beef, chicken, pork …?*
Expressions of praise and encouragement	*That's right.*
Encouraging sounds	*Uh-huh?*

5 7.4 **Practise reading Conversation B in 2 (p100) aloud.**

6 Look at transcript 7.2 **online. Find examples of encouraging independence.**

eg *Can you remember which bus we need to catch?*

Medical focus: Angina

1 Read Part 1 of the text about angina.

Angina, Part 1

In the UK, an estimated 2.3 million people live with coronary heart disease (CHD), with men significantly more at risk than women. CHD causes angina, which is very common, affecting around two million people.

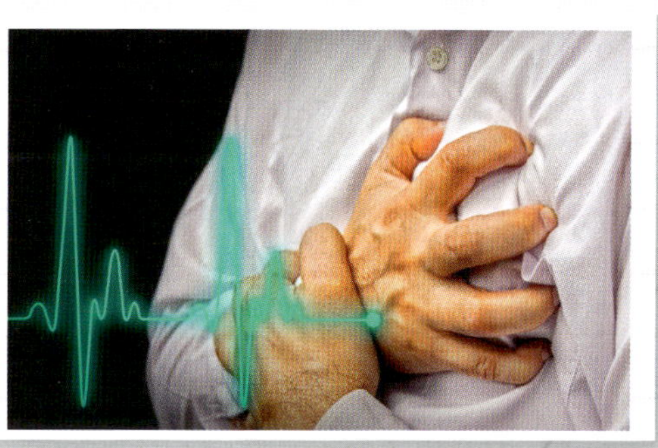

2 What do you already know about angina? Write notes under the following headings:

- Causes
- Symptoms
- Treatment

3 As you read Part 2 below, complete the blanks with the phrases in the boxes.

for a few minutes	~~a build-up of plaque~~
and widening the arteries	minutes after the second dose
heart attack or stroke	pain in the chest
don't respond to medication	and oxygen to the heart muscle
headaches, flushing and dizziness	physical activity or stress

Angina, Part 2

Causes

Most cases of angina are caused by atherosclerosis or **(a)** *a build-up of plaque* in the arteries, which restricts blood supply **(b)** ____________. Angina isn't usually life-threatening, but it can be a serious warning of a future **(c)** ____________.

Symptoms

An angina attack feels like a tight **(d)** ____________ that can sometimes spread to the left arm, neck, jaw or back. The attack only usually lasts **(e)** ____________. The main trigger is **(f)** ____________, but advanced age, smoking and obesity can also increase the risk of angina.

Treatment

Glyceryl trinitrate provides immediate relief from symptoms by relaxing **(g)** ____________, and it is available in tablet form or as a spray. There are some side effects including **(h)** ____________. If there's no improvement five **(i)** ____________, an ambulance should be called. Surgery to widen or bypass the narrowed arteries may be recommended if the symptoms **(j)** ____________.

4 Use expressions from Unit 5 (p76) to practise asking a service user about their symptoms of angina.

eg *Where does it hurt? Are you in any pain? Can you point to where it hurts?*

5 Go online and find out about how to prevent angina.

Visiting the GP

1 Read the information about Jamila. What problems do you think Jamila, who has mild learning disabilities, might have visiting the GP?

eg *Explaining her medical condition(s).*

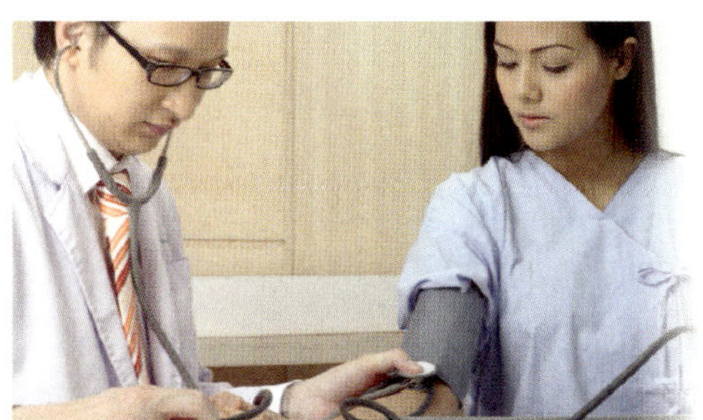

Jamila is visiting her GP. She has requested that Robert accompanies her to the appointment.

2 7.5 Listen to Part 1 and underline the correct information in *italics*.

a Jamila has a sore *eye / ear / eyelid.*

b Dr Madipali wants to use a *stethoscope / penlight (torch) / reflex hammer* to examine Jamila.

c The examination *might cause a little pain / is not painful / will be painful.*

3 7.5 Listen to Part 2 and complete Dr Madipali's expressions.

a Can you just open your eye and _______ straight ahead?

b _______ your eye open for me, please.

c Now, is it sore when I _______ your eyelid?

d How _______ have you had it for?

e It _______like something we _______ conjunctivitis. It's a minor eye _______.

4 Write Q (question), I (instruction) or E (explanation) after each expression in 3.

5 7.5 Use the words in the boxes to complete Dr Madipali's explanation of the treatment. Listen to Part 3 and check your answers.

bathe	couple	eye drops	five	flannel	prescription	warm

I'm going to give you a **(a)** _________ for some **(b)** _________. You need to put them in four times a day for the next **(c)** _________ days. Now just make sure you keep your eye clean and **(d)** _________ it with a clean **(e)** _________ and **(f)** _________ water every **(g)** _________ of hours. And don't forget to use those eye drops.

6 Rewrite the doctor's words in 5 to remind Jamila how to treat her eye infection. You can use these expressions. Then practise reminding Jamila. Remember to use a friendly tone as you speak.

- *Make sure you …*
- *Remember to …*
- *Don't forget to …*

Grammar focus: Reported speech

1 Carers sometimes need to help service users like Jamila communicate with other people. They can do this by reporting the speech of the service user or the other person. Look at these examples.

Example 1

Jamila: I have a sore eye.

Dr M: Sorry, I didn't hear you very well, Jamila. What did she say?

Robert: She said she has a sore eye.

Example 2a

Jamila: I don't have any eye drops.

Dr M: Sorry?

Robert: She said she didn't have any eye drops.

Example 2b

Jamila: I went to the doctor yesterday.

Manager: Robert, did you visit Jamila? What did she say?

Robert: She said she had been to the doctor the day before.

Example 3a

Dr M: It won't hurt.

Jamila: What?

Robert: The doctor said it wouldn't hurt.

Example 3b

Dr M: You can get the eye drops from the chemist.

Jamila: What?

Robert: The doctor said you could get the eye drops from the chemist.

2 Now read about how to report speech.

- To report information at or near the time of speaking, we can keep the *present simple* (example 1).
- To report statements, put the reported clause one tense back (eg *present simple* changes to *past simple*; *past simple* changes to *past perfect*) (examples 2a and 2b).
- If there is a time expression in what the person said, this will also change (example 2b).
- To report statements using *will*, change *will* to *would* (example 3a).
- To report statements using *can*, change *can* to *could* (example 3b).

NB: You can also add *that* eg *She said that she didn't have any eye drops..*

3 Match each time expression (a–f) to the one that would be used in reported speech (1–6).

Original speech		Reported speech	
a	this morning	1	the day before
b	today	2	the following week
c	yesterday	3	the next day
d	last week	4	that morning
e	tomorrow	5	the week before
f	next week	6	that day

4 Re-order the words in the right column to form examples of reported speech.

Original speech		Reported speech
a	*'I have a sore throat.'*	She said she / throat / sore / had a
b	*'I don't have a sore throat any more.'*	She said she / any more / have a sore throat / didn't
c	*'I also had a headache yesterday.'*	She said she had / the day before / had a headache / also
d	*'I haven't had a sore throat for a long time.'*	She said she / for a long time / a sore throat / had / hadn't
e	*'I can feel a sharp pain behind my eye.'*	She said she / behind her eye / feel a sharp pain / could
f	*'It won't hurt.'*	The doctor / hurt / it wouldn't / said

5 🔊 7.6 **Complete the dialogue to help service user Mavis communicate with her dental hygienist. Listen and check your answers.**

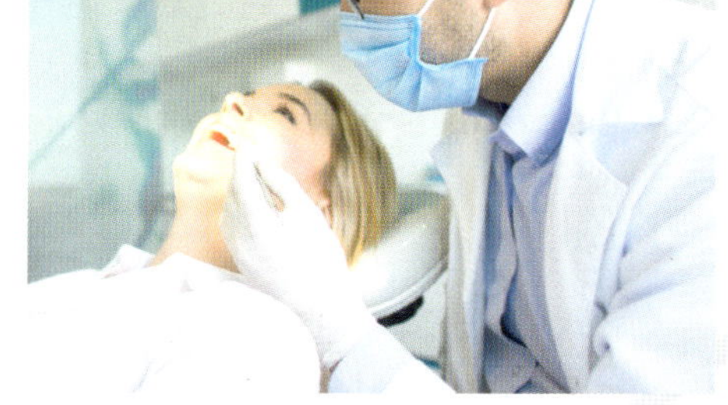

Carol: Good morning. I'm here with Mavis today. I hope that's OK.

Hygienist: Yes, of course, come in. Morning, Mavis. How are you?

Mavis: I don't like the dentist.

Hygienist: Sorry, I don't understand.

Carol: (a) ______________________________

Hygienist: Ah, but I'm not a dentist, Mavis, I'm a hygienist. You don't have to worry.

Mavis: What?

Carol: **(b)** ______________________

Mavis: What do you do then?

Hygienist: I'm just going to clean and polish your teeth. Is that OK?

Mavis: He's not a dentist, is he? What does he do?

Carol: He just told you. **(c)** ______________________

Mavis: Will it hurt?

Hygienist: No, it won't.

Mavis: It's going to hurt, isn't it, Carol?

Carol: **(d)** ______________________ Don't worry.

Hygienist: So, when was the last time you visited the dentist?

6 7.6 **Go to the transcript online. Take the role of Carol and practise using reported speech.**

Study skills (4): Listening and note-taking

1 We listen for different reasons. Tick (✓) the things you listen to in English.

	I listen to ... in English	Often	Sometimes	Not often
a	Telephone conversations			
b	Radio/online news broadcasts			
c	Audio books			
d	Information announcements (on public transport, in a shop)			
e	Lectures or presentations about social care			

2 Here are some things that might make it difficult for you to listen in English. Add three or four more to the list.

- Tone (quality of the voice)
- Difficult vocabulary
- Inability to see the speaker's face

3 Tick (✓) the techniques you would like to try.

Before attending a presentation/lecture on social care in English, I could ...

a	read about the topic in English/my own language.	
b	discuss the topic with other students.	
c	look up all the key terms and acronyms.	
d	write questions that I hope the speaker will answer.	

4 Taking notes helps us focus and understand a presentation/lecture as we listen. However, there might be a lot of information, and it is often quicker to write symbols than words or expressions. Add the symbols below to complete the table.

& = → @ ∵ ↔ ∴ +

Symbol	Meaning
+	plus, in addition to
	and
	between
	equals, is
	leads to, results in
	at
	because
	therefore

5 Match the abbreviations (a–g) to the correct meaning (1–7).

a	NB → 3	1	for example
b	no	2	approximately
c	re	3	important
d	ie	4	regarding/about
e	w/	5	number
f	c	6	that is, in other words
g	eg	7	with

6 7.7 **Susie talks about schemes to help service users remain independent. Follow these five steps.**

1 Look at the pictures and write one or two questions you would like to ask about each service.

a Handyperson service	**b** Befriending service	**c** Hospital discharge scheme

2 Listen to audio clip 7.7 and try to answer your questions.

3 Listen again and take notes, using the symbols and abbreviations in activities 4 and 5.

4 Listen again and add more detail.

5 Look at the sample answer online. Check your version with the sample and then check them both against the transcript online.

Unit 8

Safeguarding

Target areas

• Types of abuse • Dealing with disclosure • Medical focus: Dementia • Reporting abuse allegations • Relative clauses (*who*, *which*, *that*) • Report writing (4)

In their shoes

1 Read these comments about abuse. Do you agree? Why (not)?

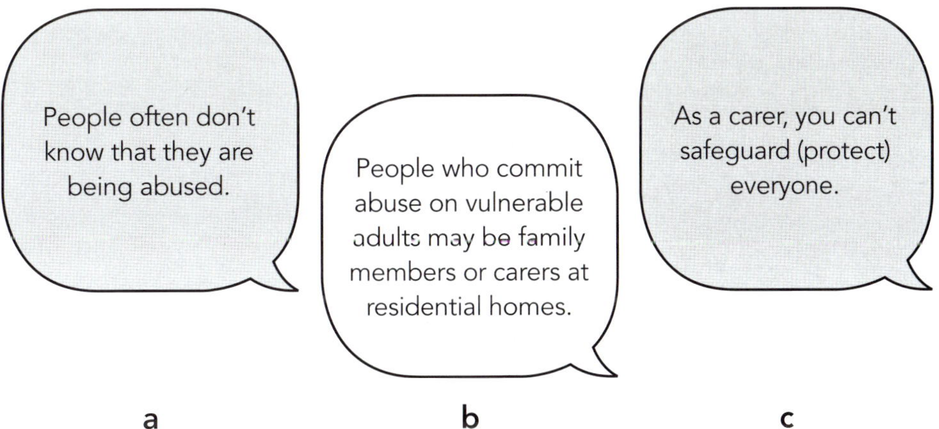

2 Write two or three steps you would take to stop the abuse of the service users you care for.

eg *Report your concerns about the service user to your supervisor.*

Types of abuse

1 Label the types of abuse that might be taking place in the scenarios described below. Use the words in the boxes.

physical	financial	psychological (or emotional)

a Mr Allen (94) is a widower living alone. His son takes care of him, assisted by a carer. The carer has noticed objects of value have recently disappeared from the house.	**b** Neighbours frequently hear shouting and screaming coming from Sian's flat. Sian (53) has a learning disability. Her unemployed brother lives with her.	**c** Carer Anya has noticed bruising on Dottie's arms and legs. Dottie (87) suffers from severe arthritis. Her husband Reg (88) now struggles to care for his wife.
__________ **abuse**	__________ **abuse**	__________ **abuse**

2 Match the description (a–d) to the correct type of abuse (1–4).

	Type of abuse		Description
a	Sexual abuse occurs when → 3	1	there is a focus on the needs of the organisation and not those of the service users.
b	Discriminatory abuse is when	2	a carer fails to provide the basic needs (eg personal hygiene care) for someone.
c	Neglect is when	3	sexual activity is forced on someone without his or her consent.
d	Institutional abuse occurs when	4	someone is treated unequally because of their age, gender, race, sexual orientation or disability.

3 Give two or three more examples of institutional abuse. Give two or three examples of neglect.

eg institutional abuse: *restricting (limiting) visiting hours at a residential care home*

4 Add vowels (*a, e, i, o, u*) to complete these typical signs of abuse.

a	s_res around the g_n_tal area, s_x_ally tr_nsm_tted _nf_ctions (STIs), pr_gn_ncy	*sexual abuse*
b	_np_id bills, _mpty fo_d c_pb_ards, items m_ssing from the home	
c	br_ken b_nes, br_is_s, b_tes, b_rn m_rks	
d	b_ds_res, m_ln_trition, d_hydr_tion, d_rty cl_thing and b_dding	
e	anxi_ty, l_w s_lf-est_em, l_ck of sl_ ep	

5 Write the correct abuse type for each set of examples in 4.

6 🔊 8.1 **You're going to hear a carer discussing service users Ian and Mark. Listen and tick (✓) the injuries for each service user.**

a Ian

Pressure sores		Excoriation, red areas (not broken down)	
Bruising		Scalds, burns	
Cuts, wounds		Other (specify)	

a Mark

Pressure sores		Excoriation, red areas (not broken down)	
Bruising		Scalds, burns	
Cuts, wounds		Other (specify)	

7 🔊 8.1 **Listen again and complete the body map for each service user.**

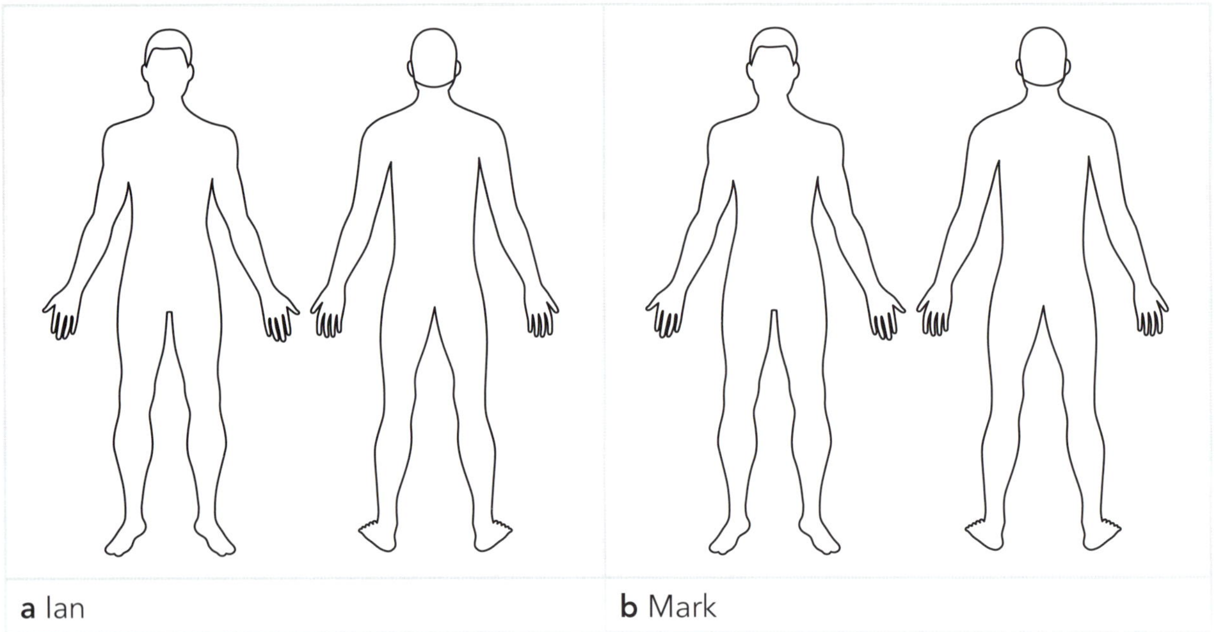

8 🔊 8.1 **Match the two halves to complete the carers' sentences. Then listen and check your answers.**

a	He was → 3	1	new pressure sore, I'm afraid.
b	He's got	2	nurse to look at that.
c	It looks like someone has tried to	3	covered in bruises.
d	It looks like you've got a	4	bruises on his upper arms.
e	It looks	5	pull him out of his chair.
f	We'll ask the	6	painful.

9 🔊 8.2 **Listen and practise saying the sentences in 8 aloud.**

Dealing with disclosure

1 Read about service user Peddy Singh. Which type(s) of abuse should Christiana watch for when caring for Peddy?

Peddy (47), who is diagnosed with a mental health disorder, lives on her own in the community. She is supported for two hours a day by Christiana, a rehab support worker.

2 🔊 8.3 **Listen and write *T* (true) or *F* (false) for each statement.**

a	Peddy is very talkative today.	*F*
b	Christiana needs to understand the situation so she can help Peddy.	
c	Peddy is embarrassed about the situation.	
d	Billy tried to follow Peddy and take her to his room.	
e	Christiana has Peddy's consent to report the incident.	

3 Correct the false statements in 2. Which type(s) of abuse has Peddy suffered?

4 🔊 8.3 **Match the two halves to form Christiana's expressions. Listen and check your answers.**

a	If there's something wrong, → 2	1	tell me what happened with Billy.
b	Why don't you start at the beginning and tell	2	you can always speak to me.
c	I can help you, but	3	me exactly what happened?
d	Just try to relax and	4	did the right thing.
e	It must have been	5	only if you explain the situation to me.
f	Thank you for telling me. You	6	really frightening.

5 🔊 8.3 **Listen again and number the events of the incident in the correct order (1–7).**

a	He put his hand on her breast and kissed her hard on the cheek.	
b	Billy came in and sat down next to her.	
c	She managed to push him away.	
d	He then suggested they go upstairs.	
e	It was about 11.30 and Peddy was sitting in the day room.	*1*
f	She ran home.	
g	He put his arm around her.	

6 Add vowels (*a, e, i, o, u*) to complete Christiana's request for consent.

I n_ed y_ur p_rm_ssi_n to r_p_rt th_s to my s_ni_r m_n_g_r.

7 8.4 **Listen and repeat Christiana's sentences in 4. Follow the correct intonation pattern – your voice should go up and down as you speak.**

8 Read these guidelines for carers. Check any new words in a dictionary.

If a service user tells you he/she has been abused:

a Reassure the service user you will take what they say seriously.

b Help the service user explain the details of the incident.

c Explain that you cannot promise to keep the incident a secret.

d Explain that it is your duty to protect the service user.

e Listen carefully to what the service user is saying.

f Reassure the service user that they will be involved in decisions about the incident.

g Do not be judgemental or jump to conclusions.

(Adapted from Care Certificate Workbook)

9 Read transcript 8.3 **online and tick (✓) the guidelines Christiana followed.**

a ☐ b ☐ c ☐ d ☐ e ☐ f ☐ g ☐

10 Read about service user David.

David (25), who has a learning disability, lives on his own in a supported living flat. He is assisted for three hours a day by his support worker, Jacob.

11 David tells Jacob about a distressing incident. Look at what Jacob says. Write a letter (a–g) for each of the guidelines in 8.

a I'm afraid I can't make promises.

b It's my job to report incidents like this to the management team.

c Do you want to tell me more?

d I want to try to help you, David, but you need to tell me exactly what happened.

12 🔊 8.5 **Use the expressions from 11 to complete the dialogue. Then listen to Part 1 and check your answers.**

Jacob: You look upset, David. What is it?

David: Well, it happened when I was walking home from the day centre yesterday.

Jacob: What happened, David? **(a)** ____________________

David: Yes, but they told me not to tell anybody or they'd hit me!

Jacob: **(b)** ____________________.

David: Yes, I'll tell you, but you must promise you won't tell anybody else. I don't want to get them in any trouble.

Jacob: David, **(c)** ____________________. **(d)** ____________________. Now, if you tell me what happened, I'll help you and we can sort this out together. How does that sound?

13 Which type(s) of abuse do you think has David suffered?

14 <u>Underline</u> the expression in 12 that Jacob uses to ask for consent.

15 🔊 8.5 **Listen to Part 2. <u>Underline</u> the correct information in *italics*.**

a David was attacked by two boys who *hit him / stole his money*.

b David was *very badly* hurt / *not badly*.

c David is worried the boys will *attack him again / go to the police*.

d Jacob is going to report the incident to *his manager / the police*.

16 🖥 **Look at the transcript for Part 2 online and answer these questions.**

a Which two expressions does Jacob use to encourage David to tell his story?

b What does Jacob say to reassure David?

Medical focus: Dementia

1 Read Part 1 of the text about dementia. Fill in the gaps with the numbers in the boxes. How is dementia categorised?

one million	2021	65	800,000	two-thirds

Dementia, Part 1

Introduction: The UK's Alzheimer's Society estimate that by **(a)** ________, around **(b)** ________ people will suffer from dementia. Approximately **(c)** ________ people in the UK currently live with dementia; **(d)** ________ are women and one third are over **(e)** ________.

Causes: Dementia is not classed as a disease, but a collection of symptoms caused by various diseases. These include Alzheimer's disease and vascular dementia.

2 Write down three or four symptoms that you think are experienced by service users with dementia. Then read Part 2 of the text and check your answers.

eg *memory loss*

Part 2

Symptoms: Memory loss is the most well-known symptom of Alzheimer's, but service users with dementia might also have difficulty with language and become confused in unfamiliar situations. They may also suffer from depression, changes in personality and hallucinations. Symptoms of Alzheimer's may not be immediately noticeable. However, with time, service users will neglect their health and nutrition and may also experience incontinence and increased difficulties with mobility. For those with vascular dementia, symptoms may develop very suddenly. These service users may also experience stroke-like symptoms, including muscle weakness or paralysis on one side of their body.

3 Read Part 3 and write *T* (true) or *F* (false) for each of the statements that follow.

Part 3

Treatment: Dementia is not curable, but some medications can be effective in treating hallucinations, although they may also produce side effects, such as nausea and sickness and even slowing down of the heartbeat. Anti-depressants may also be prescribed, but most dementia patients respond well to cognitive stimulation by taking part in activities to improve their memory as well as problem-solving and activities which develop their language skills. Finally, reality orientation therapy helps reduce feelings of memory loss and confusion, although the benefits are small.

a Certain medications can cure dementia.

b Medication for dementia can cause nausea and slowing of the heartbeat.

c Service users with dementia might find cognitive stimulation beneficial.

d Reality orientation therapy is very effective in treating memory loss and confusion.

4 Correct the false statements in 3.

5 Practise describing treatment options for dementia to a new carer you are supervising. Use the information in Parts 1 to 3 about dementia.

6 Go online and find out more about ...

- Alzheimer's disease
- Vascular dementia

Reporting an abuse allegation

1 Use the words in the boxes to complete the definitions.

accusation/ allegation	incident form	sexual advance	sexual assault

a ______________: an attempt to have a sexual relationship with someone that is sometimes unwanted.

b ______________: a suggestion that someone has done something wrong or illegal, but without proof.

c ____________: a document used to report something that has happened.

d ____________: an attack with a sexual motivation.

2 What do you think is the difference between rape and sexual assault?

3 Read these definitions and check your answers to 2.

> *Rape* is when someone has penetrative sex with another person against their will. This includes vaginal, anal and oral penetration.
>
> *Sexual assault* covers any other sort of sexual contact and behaviour that is unwanted, ranging from touching to any other activity if it is sexual.

Source: http://www.nidirect.gov.uk/sv-definition (accessed October 2016).

4 Read about Christiana. Think about your own work situation. What steps would you take in order to report an abuse allegation?

Christiana is reporting an abuse allegation to her manager, Mo.

5 🔊 8.6 **Christiana is reporting the incident to Mo. Use the terms from 1 to complete Christiana's expressions. Listen and check your answers.**

I need to talk to you about a serious **(a)** ________ made by one of my service users. It's Peddy Singh. I was with her this morning. She made an **(b)** ________ of **(c)** ________against Billy Morgan, one of the service users at the outreach centre. I've filled out an **(d)** ________.

6 Read the case study and complete the body map.

Case study

Rezaur is Danny's key support worker. Every morning he helps Danny get out of bed and supports him with personal care. Rezaur has been on holiday for two weeks. On his return, Rezaur visits Danny. As he enters the room, the first thing he notices is the strong smell of urine. The room is untidy, there are clothes all over the floor and both the curtains and the window have been left open. It is a cold autumn morning, but Danny is lying naked and there are no covers on his bed. Rezaur also notices that Danny is shivering and he has a large bruise around the front of each upper arm and a minor pressure sore on his right buttock.

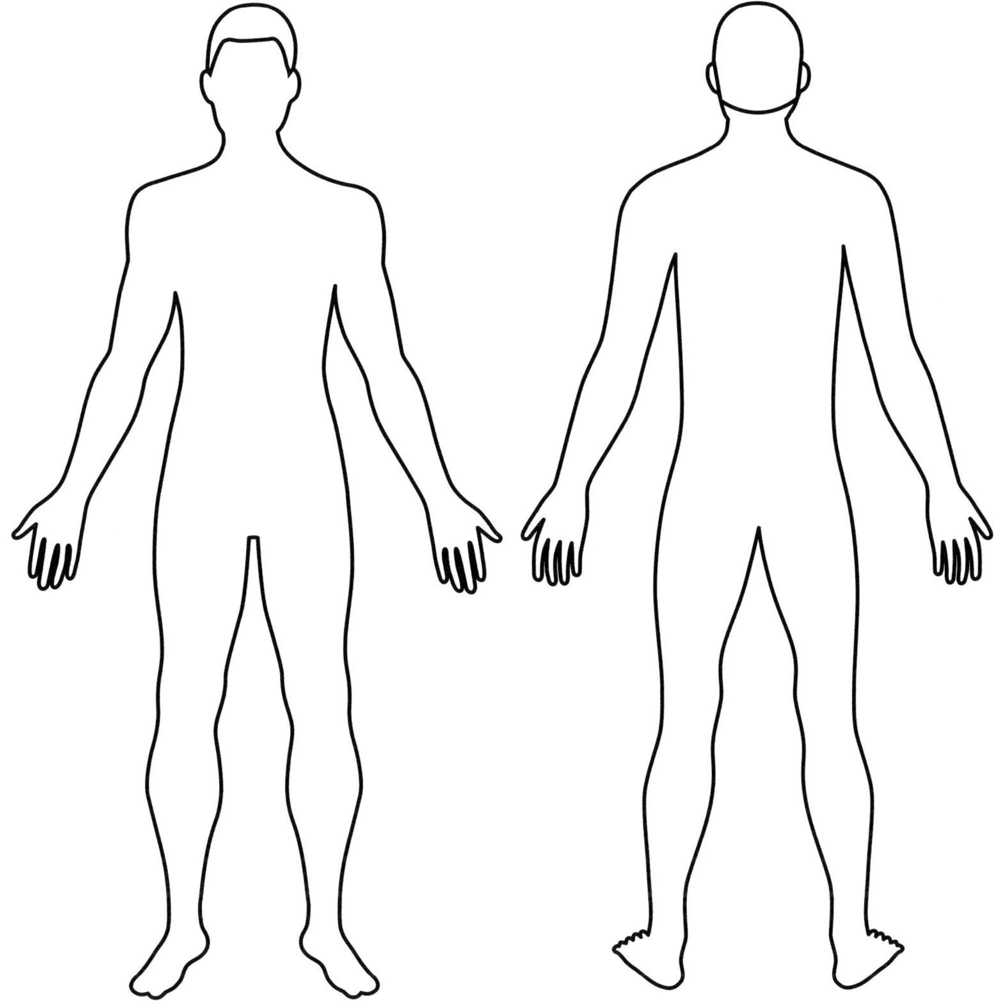

7 Read the case study again and answer these questions.

a What type(s) of abuse has Danny suffered?

b How do you think this might have happened?

c How would you reassure Danny? What would you say and do?

8 Report the incident in 6 to your manager. Write a dialogue using this manager's questions to help you.

- ▶ *How can I help you?*
- ▶ *So what's been happening?*
- ▶ *Can you just go through it with me, please?*
- ▶ *How is Danny now?*
- ▶ *I'm going to look into it immediately. In the meantime, can you reassure him that we're investigating the case?*

Grammar focus: relative clauses (*who, which, that*)

1 Read about relative clauses.

We use a relative clause to link two sentences together. We use *who, which* and *that* instead of nouns and pronouns (*he, she, it, they)* in the second sentence.		
1	We use *who* to talk about people (replaces *he/she/they*)	eg Carol cares for Ms Bridges. She lives nearby. → Carol cares for Ms Bridges *who* lives nearby.
2	We use *which* or *that* to talk about things (replaces *it/they*).	eg Where is my apron? It was in the cupboard. → Where is my apron *which* was in the cupboard? This is the apron. I was looking for it. → This is the apron *that* I was looking for.

2 Correct these sentences, if necessary.

a Sylvie which usually cares for me is away on holiday this week.
eg *Sylvie, who usually cares for me, is away on holiday this week.*

b She took the medication who was on the table by mistake.

c Have you taken all the antibiotics what your doctor prescribed?

d An antibiotic is a medication that fights bacterial not viral infection.

e I sometimes have carers who they come from Poland.

3 Choose the correct word (*who, which* or *that*) to complete the report for service user Alex.

Daily Care Report		SunnyView CARE	
Date am/pm	**Observations** *(please include information such as personal care given, food eaten, general mood and state of service user etc.)*	**Name of carer**	**Signature of carer**
15.01.16 pm	On arrival, Alex, (a) ________ seemed a little down, told me that she had a UTI. She is now on antibiotics (b) ________ need to be given three times a day. Her daughter-in-law will stay overnight with Alex. She says she will dispense the lunchtime dose. I have also informed the office of the diagnosis and the medication. I helped Alex choose her dinner. She chose a beef stew ready meal (c) ________ she really enjoyed. Evening medication given and signed for. I also checked her bedsheets, (e) ________ were dry and clean. No other issues to report.	Pauline Weller	P. Weller

Report writing (4)

1 Add the adjectives in the boxes to complete Christiana's report about Peddy. What do you think the expression 'she didn't seem herself' means?

angry (x2)	cheerful	quiet	sad	talkative

Daily Care Report — SunnyView CARE

Date am/pm	Observations (please include information such as personal care given, food eaten, general mood and state of service user etc.)	Name of carer	Signature of carer
20.04.16	Peddy was still in bed when I arrived today at 12.30. She's usually quite (a) ______ and wants to tell me everything about her life, but today she was (b) ______ and I could hardly get a word out of her. She didn't seem herself. Encouraged her to take a shower and freshen up. Prepared lunch (tuna salad sandwich), but she only ate half. Chatted about the previous day. Peddy talked about an incident at the outreach centre that she was extremely (c) ______ about. She's still (d) ______ but has agreed for me to report the incident. Kitchen and bathroom tidied and cleaned. Medication dispensed and signed for. Reminded her I was moving to London and today was my last day. Peddy seemed a little (e) ______ about that. Wrote the name of the new carer in her memory book. (Kelly – Could you please help Peddy make an appointment with her GP on Monday? Thanks.) When I left, Peddy was in a more (f) ______ mood. Informed the office of incident at outreach centre. No other issues to report.	Christiana	Christiana

2 Cover the report in 1 and complete Christiana's actions. Use the correct verb in the past simple. Read the report again and check your answers.

a *Encouraged* her to take a shower and freshen up.

b P__________ lunch (tuna salad sandwich), but she only ate half.

c C__________ about the previous day.

d Kitchen and bathroom t__________ and c__________.

e Medication d__________ and s__________ for.

f R___________ her I was moving to London.

g W___________ the name of the new carer in her memory book.

h I___________ the office of incident at outreach centre.

3 Think of a service user you know and write the report for the last time you visited him/her. Include information about the service user's mood and the actions you took.

Daily Care Report			SunnyView CARE
Date am/ pm	**Observations** *(please include information such as personal care given, food eaten, general mood and state of service user etc.)*	**Name of carer**	**Signature of carer**
20.04.16			

Unit 9

Challenging situations

Target areas

• Recognising and acknowledging emotional states • Demonstrating empathy
• Types of challenging behaviour • De-escalating a challenging situation
• Conditionals • Medical focus: Autism Spectrum Disorder • Completing an ABC chart

In their shoes

1 What causes people to feel distressed? Use the expressions in the boxes to label the pictures.

being overworked	crowded spaces	financial worries
death of a close friend or relative	relationship problems	~~serious family illness~~

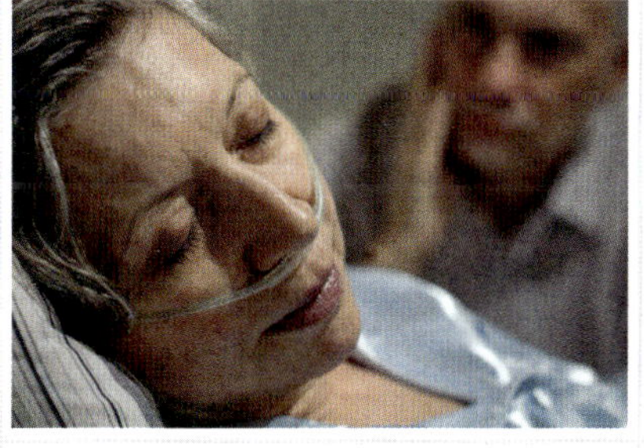

a *serious family illness*

b ___________

c ___________

d ___________

e ___________

f ___________

2 Write two or three other possible causes of distress.

3 Write two or three adjectives to describe how you would feel in the situations in 1.

4 Think about these questions.

a In your country, in which situations is it acceptable to cry or express anger in public?

b How easily do/would you deal with service users expressing emotions in these situations?

c How easily do you hide your emotions?

Recognising and acknowledging emotional states

1 Label the pictures with two or more adjectives to describe the emotions of these service users.

~~angry~~	annoyed	bored	cross	depressed	discontented
down	furious	irritated	miserable	sad	tired
unhappy	upset	weary	withdrawn		

a Sylvia ______________	**b** Daphne______________	**c** Rana *angry*

2 🔊 9.1 Listen and write the correct adjective for each service user.

a Sylvia ______________ **b** Daphne______________ **c** Rana ______________

3 🔊 9.1 Listen again. Complete the carers' expressions for acknowledging the service users' emotions.

a You sound ______.

b You ______ very ______.

c You seem ______.

4 Re-order these words to form expressions about emotions. Is the speaker in each case busy or depressed/sad?

a my plate / a lot / have / I / on

b falling / apart / is just / life / my

c mess / a / everything's / such

5 Look at how carers ask service users for clarification.

a What do you mean by 'falling apart'?

b You say 'falling apart'; what do you mean?

c Why do you think you're falling apart?

6 Practise asking service users for clarification of the expressions in 4. Use the underlined language in 5.

Demonstrating empathy

1 Read some information about Enid. What aspect(s) of Enid's emotional well-being should Mary (her domiciliary care worker) look out for?

2 9.2 **Listen to Part 1 and underline the correct words in *italics* to complete the statements.**

a The film reminded Enid of her *husband / father / son*.

b Enid is worried that Mary will find her family story too *long / sad / boring*.

c Mary's husband is *exactly like / totally unlike / similar to* George.

d George was *a history / an English / a maths* teacher.

e Many of George's *school friends / colleagues / students* attended his funeral.

3 🔊 9.2 **Listen again and complete Mary's sentences. Then answer the question that follows.**

a ________ a little down. ________, Enid?
b I know you ___________.
c I am here ___________.
d __________, what did he do?
e ___________ so proud of him.

Why do you think Mary starts her question with 'Remind me, …'?

4 🔊 9.2 **Listen to Part 2. Write *T* (true) or *F* (false) for each statement. Correct the false statements.**

a George died of pancreatic cancer.
b George died at home.
c At first, Enid does not want to talk to anyone else about her emotions.
d Mary promises to ask someone at the day centre to contact Enid.

5 🔊 9.2 **Add vowels (*a, e, i, o, u*) to form Mary's questions and statements. Then listen and check your answers.**

a If you d_n't mind me _sking, h_w d_d he d_e?
b It m_st h_ve b_en h_rd to w_tch him s_ffer.
c H_w _re y_u fe_ling n_w?
d M_ybe s_me_ne c_n c_me and ke_p you c_mp_ny.

6 Re-order the words to form Mary's request for consent.

to someone / about your feelings? / How / talking / would you feel about

7 We can show empathy like this.

It/This/That/He/She/They must be + noun/adjective

eg *This must be a* <u>*shock*</u> *for you. It must have been* <u>*difficult*</u> *for you.*

8 Complete these expressions of empathy for talking about the present and the past.

a That ___________ awful.
eg *That must be awful. That must have been awful.*
b You ___________ so proud of him.
c He ____________ in real pain.
d It ______________ hard to watch him suffer.

9 9.3 **Listen and repeat what you hear. (Practise sitting with an open posture as you speak – don't fold your arms or cross your legs. Smile and imagine making eye contact with the service user.)**

- **a** You look a little down. What's wrong?
- **b** Remind me, what did he do?
- **c** If you don't mind me asking, how did he die?
- **d** You must have been very proud of him.
- **e** It must have been very hard to watch him suffer.

10 Complete the conversations with these service users by adding an expression of empathy.

a Sylvia

Carer: You sound quite depressed, Sylvia.
Sylvia: I am. I feel my life is just falling apart.
Carer: What do you mean by 'falling apart'?
Sylvia: My sister passed away last week. We were so close.
Carer: ______________________________

b Daphne

Carer: You look very tired, Daphne
Daphne: I have a lot on my plate at the moment.
Carer: You say you have 'a lot on your plate'. What do you mean?
Daphne: I have an appointment at the hospital this afternoon. My son is coming round with the grandchildren, and I haven't managed to do the cleaning or the shopping. I'm so …
Carer: ______________________________

a Rana

Carer: You seem angry about something, Rana.
Rana: Everything is such a mess.
Carer: Why do you think everything's a mess?
Rana: You know, my mum didn't come to the meeting at the bank today. She promised. So now I'm in real trouble.
Carer: ______________________________

11 Practise reading the conversations in 10 aloud.

Types of challenging behaviour

1 Put these examples of challenging behaviour under the correct headings.

NB. they may appear under more than one heading.

hitting, biting	pinching	tapping something on the table	
throwing objects	rocking	verbal abuse (shouting, insulting words, swearing)	
head banging	pushing	drawing on walls/books	loud humming

Aggression towards another person	Self-injury	Destruction	Other
hitting			

2 Think about service users you know. What kind(s) of challenging behaviour do they demonstrate?

3 We can divide reasons for challenging behaviour into four groups. As you read, write the missing cause for each paragraph.

Escape (E)	Sensory (S)	Social attention (SA)	Tangibles (real) (T)

As a carer, it's important to understand the reasons for challenging behaviour.

(a) ___________ is one reason. The service user may have limited communication skills or just be bored. By behaving in a certain way, he learns he can attract the attention of another person, either negatively or positively.

(b) ___________ is another type of learned behaviour. If the service user wants something – food, drink, an object – he knows he can use challenging behaviour to get what he wants.

(c) ___________ is where service users demonstrate challenging behaviour to avoid or get away from certain situations or activities they don't want to do or don't find interesting.

(d) ___________ is the fourth reason. This is when the person uses behaviour they find enjoyable or rewarding, such as tapping a pencil on a table. The service user likes the sound and this is more important than what is happening around him.

(Adapted from Challenging Behaviour Foundation (accessed November 2015)) www.challengingbehaviour.org.uk

4 🔊 9.4 **Trainer Michael is talking about children with learning disabilities. Listen and write the reason (*E*, *S*, *SA* or *T*) for each child's challenging behaviour.**

a Khalid ______	**b** Rowen ______	**c** Carmella ______	**d** Helen ______

5 🔊 9.4 **Listen again and complete the students' notes.**

Name		**What does he/she do?**	**Why?**
a	Khalid	*Rocks* in chair, ______ loudly	He's *bored*.
b	Rowen	______ himself	He likes individual attention ______.
c	Carmella	______ another child	She prefers to be ______.
d	Helen	______ a dish at her teacher	She's ______.

De-escalating a challenging situation

1 **Here is some advice for de-escalating (calming down) challenging situations. Write three or four more ideas.**

- Stay calm.
- Use clear, firm language.
- Ask the service user to sit down.
- Don't get defensive. (Don't give the impression of being unsure/threatened.)

2 **Here are six steps for de-escalating a challenging situation. Number them in the correct order (1–6).**

a	Repeat back the issue(s) to the service user.		d	Empathise with the service user.	
b	Clarify the cause of the anger.		e	Summarise the options.	
c	Plan a course of action together.		f	Acknowledge the service user's anger.	*1*

3 Read about service user Bala. What do you think could be the reason(s) for Bala's challenging behaviour?

Bala Patel (19) has learning difficulties and lives in a supported living flat. His carer, Tunde, a community outreach worker for people with learning disabilities, visits him regularly. Bala occasionally demonstrates challenging behaviour.

4 9.5 **Listen to Part 1 of a conversation between Bala and Tunde. Complete the table about Bala.**

What does he do?	Why?	Reason for behaviour *(circle one)*
		E S SA T

5 9.5 **Listen to Part 2 and underline the words in *italics* to complete the statements.**

a Bala's mother was upset that Bala had *bought / been watching / thrown away* lots of DVDs.

b Tunde *tries to calm Bala down / shouts at Bala / stops Bala from buying more DVDs.*

c Tunde explains *the policy on challenging behaviour / that Bala is going to lose his accommodation.*

d Bala *continues shouting / apologises to Tunde / says he will apologise to his mother.*

6 9.5 **Listen to Parts 1 and 2 again. Tick the steps from 2 that Tunde uses to de-escalate the situation.**

Step 1 ☐ Step 2 ☐ Step 3 ☐ Step 4 ☐

Step 5 ☐ Step 6 ☐

7 Read transcript 9.5 **online. Find examples for each of the steps in 6.**

eg Step 1: *I can see you're angry.*

8 🔊 9.6 **Listen and practise saying Tunde's sentences aloud. Speak calmly and clearly.**

a I need you to take a step back and calm down.

b Why don't we go inside, sit down and talk about this?

c I want you to tell me what the problem is without shouting or getting upset.

d Sometimes you have to listen to people, even if it's something you don't want to hear.

9 Some carers ask service users to keep a diary of their feelings. How do you think keeping a diary of feelings could help a service user? What sort of things do you think service users could include in the diary?

Completing an ABC chart

1 Look at the ABC (Antecedent, Behaviour, Consequence) chart. Then, in the sentences that follow, underline the words in *italics* to complete the definitions.

ABC chart	SunnyView CARE
Name:	Maria Matheson
Date and time of incident:	19.01.2016 / 16.45
Description of behaviour:	Maria kicked and punched a member of staff at the care home.
Antecedent events:	Maria received a call to say her father was not coming to visit as originally planned.
Consequent events:	Member of staff who has been attacked is asked to leave the room. Maria is asked to calm down and sit with the lead member of staff. Maria is offered a cold drink and asked to explain her actions, explaining what has happened and why.
Signature:	Maria Matheson

a *Antecedent events / Consequent events* take place after the incident reported by the carer.

b *Antecedent events / Consequent events* take place before the incident reported by the carer.

2 Answer these questions.

a When do carers use ABC charts?

b What is your experience using ABC charts?

3 Use the expressions in the boxes to complete the ABC chart for Youssef.

had spoiled his own day	escorted Youssef out of the cafe
having a drink and a sandwich	talked about his behaviour
coffee spilt over the table	~~a member of the public~~
calmed down	

ABC chart — *SunnyView* CARE

Name:	Amit Ghosh
Date and time of incident:	4/11/2016 at 13:45
Description of behaviour:	Youssef shouted threatening language at **(a)** *a member of the public* in a cafe in town.
Antecedent events:	Youssef was sitting with me (Amit) in a cafe **(b)** ___________. The café was busy and noisy. A member of the public knocked the table where Youssef was sitting and his **(c)** ___________.
Consequent events	I (Amit) **(d)** ___________. We sat on a bench while Youssef **(e)** ___________. We **(f)** ___________and how it was unacceptable. Youssef agreed that he **(g)** ___________. We then went home early.
Signature:	Amit Ghosh

4 Answer these questions.

a What technique did Amit use to de-escalate the situation?

b Was Amit's de-escalation technique successful? Why (not)?

5 Now complete the ABC chart for Bala (p133). Re-read transcript 9.5 online to remind yourself of the conversation with Bala, if necessary.

REMEMBER

Always sign and date all documents.

Always clarify who is speaking eg *I (Amit), me (Amit), myself (Amit)* **to avoid misunderstanding.**

ABC chart

SunnyView CARE

Name: Bala Patel

Date and time of incident:

Description of behaviour:

Antecedent events:

Consequent events:

Signature: Tunde Bakare

Grammar focus: Conditionals

1 Read how we use conditionals.

1 Use *if* + present simple + present simple to talk about facts, recommendations or actions.	*If you have questions about your care plan, speak to your case manager.*
2 Use *if* + present simple + *will* to talk about real situations or situations that will probably occur.	*If Tony needs more help with his ADLs, he'll tell us.*
NB. You can change the order of these sentences. You can use *when* instead of *if*.	*Tony will tell us if he needs more help with his ADLs.* *When Tony needs more help with his ADLs, he'll tell us.*

2 Read transcript 9.5 online. Find three examples of conditionals.

eg *If you don't have enough money, you have to borrow from your mum, don't you?*

3 Use the verbs in brackets to complete these examples of conditionals. You may need to change the verb form.

a If Youssef is aggressive to someone again, _______ him to apologise to the person immediately. (~~*be*~~ */ ask*)

b Youssef often becomes aggressive, when he _______ threatened. (~~*become*~~ */ feel*)

c If Amit _______ quickly, Youssef _______possibly _______ physical violence. (not / *act / use*)

d It_______ better if Amit _______ taking Youssef to busy cafes and restaurants. (*be / avoid*)

e When Amit _______ to Youssef quietly and calmly, he _______ being aggressive. (*talk / stop*)

f If you _______ advice on dealing with challenging behaviour, _______ to your supervisor. (*need / speak*)

4 Complete the dialogues (a–d) between carers and supervisors about challenging behaviour, using the sentences in the box.

We can advise you about courses that are available, if you like.
Well, if that happens, then you need to leave the room and ask a colleague to help you.
If he gets angry, just follow the six steps for de-escalating challenging situations.
If his behaviour doesn't improve, he may lose his accommodation.

a

Carer: What if my service user becomes angry again?

Supervisor: ______________________________

b

Carer: And how about if he becomes violent?

Supervisor: ______________________________

c

Carer: What if he still continues to show challenging behaviour?

Supervisor: ______________________________

d

Carer: How can I develop my skills?

Supervisor: ______________________________

Medical focus: Autism Spectrum Disorder

1 Read the statements about Autism Spectrum Disorder (ASD). From your own knowledge of ASD, do you agree or disagree (✓) with the statements?

		Agree	Disagree
a	More girls are diagnosed with ASD than boys.		
b	There is no 'cure' for ASD.		
c	Autism is classed as a learning disability.		
d	The causes of ASD are still being investigated.		
e	Down's syndrome may be a cause of ASD in some cases.		

2 📖 Read the following text and check your answers to 1.

Living with autism

What causes autism?

Although scientists know that autism is more common in boys than girls, they still don't know the exact causes of the condition. However, there is strong evidence to suggest it is caused by environmental and neurological factors that affect development of the brain. Certain conditions, such as tuberous sclerosis (a rare genetic condition causing non-cancerous tumours in the brain) and Down's syndrome, are also known to increase the risk of ASD. Although there is no cure for the condition, some treatments, including psychological therapy and medication, can help.

3 Complete Part 2 of the text using the expressions in the boxes.

smell or colour	routine and solitude	~~social interaction~~
obsessive interest	above-average intelligence	exceptionally talented
tone of voice	facial expressions	

What are the main characteristics of autism?

Typically, people with autism find communication and **(a)** _social interaction_ difficult. They often don't understand verbal messages (in particular **(b)** ____________, jokes and sarcasm) and non-verbal language (eg gestures and **(c)** ____________), and they are unable to recognise the feelings of others. They find the world confusing and unpredictable, preferring **(d)** ____________. They may also suffer from sensitivity to sound, light, **(e)** ____________.

What is Asperger's syndrome?

Asperger's syndrome is the best-known form of autism. Those with the condition often have average or **(f)** ____________. Some develop an almost **(g)** ____________ in a specific area – maps, mathematics etc., and a minority are **(h)** ____________.

4 Go online and find out about other mental health issues.

- Bipolar disorder
- Attention Deficit Hyperactivity Disorder (ADHD)
- Depression

Unit 10

Personal and professional development

Target areas

• Describing attributes •Talking about career pathways •Applying for a job in social care • Answering typical interview questions • Attending supervision • Receiving feedback • Continued professional development (CPD) • Completing a language action plan

In their shoes

1 Read this description of someone's ideal carer. Who do you think made the comment?

'If that was my grandmother, how would I like them to be looked after? If carers follow that pattern, they can't go wrong, can they?'

2 🔊 10.1 **Doris and Brian describe their ideal carers. Listen and write down the adjectives they use.**

a Doris

c Brian

3 Write a short description of your ideal carer (20 words maximum).

Describing attributes

1 Match the attributes (a–h) for a good carer to the correct synonym (1–8).

a	caring → 5	1	structured
b	honest	2	adaptable
c	non-judgemental	3	happy
d	sympathetic	4	understanding
e	cheerful	5	kind
f	flexible	6	friendly
g	approachable	7	truthful
h	organised	8	open-minded

2 Sometimes we can create opposites of adjectives by adding a prefix, such as *un*, *dis* or *in*. Use these prefixes to create opposites for some of the attributes in 1.

eg *uncaring*

3 Add one verb to form four more attributes. Check any new words in a dictionary.

___ a sense of humour

___ integrity

___ good listening skills

___ good time management skills

NB. You can also use the more formal verb *possess* eg *I possess good listening skills.*

5 Write a list of your attributes. Practise answering the opening question of an interview. You might want to begin like this:

Interviewer: Tell us about yourself.

You: I'm …. / I think of myself as … / I consider myself to be …

Talking about career pathways

Nadia

Dan

1 🔊 10.2 **Nadia and Dan talk about their career pathways. Listen and tick (✓) the attributes they mention.**

Nadia:	patient	☐	flexible	☐	honest	☐
	adaptable	☐	kind	☐		
Dan:	caring	☐	organised	☐	cheerful	☐
	open-minded	☐	non-judgemental	☐		

2 🔊 10.2 **Combine the words in the box to form job titles. Then listen and plot Nadia and Dan's career pathway and career goals.**

~~assistant~~, ~~care~~, leader, manager, senior, social, support, support, support, team, worker, worker, worker

Nadia

Career pathway: *care assistant* → ________________

Career goal: ________________

Dan

Career pathway: ________________ → ________________

Career goal: ________________

3 **Match the terms a–g below, which we use to talk about career pathways, to the correct definitions (1–7).**

a	vacancy → 3	1	job
b	transferable skills	2	when something is recognised officially
c	an appraisal	3	a job that no one is doing at the moment, and which is available
d	supervisor	4	someone who watches another person to check they are doing their job properly
e	post	5	skills used in one job that can also be used in another
f	accredited	6	to do a completely different job
g	make a career change	7	a meeting to discuss someone's progress

4 As you read about carer Jackie Davies, complete the text with some of the terms in 3. What transferable skills do you think Jackie possesses?

Jackie Davies

I entered the care field ten years ago as a support worker. I had decided to make a **(a)** *career change* – I was a teacher before, so I had a lot of **(b)** ___________. Working with young people with learning disabilities is challenging, but rewarding at the same time. I love working in partnership with people and helping them achieve their goals. I've attended some **(c)** _____________ training sessions, including manual handling and safeguarding adults. Then in 2014 I took my Level 3 Diploma in Health and Social Care, which really helped improve my confidence. Last year, my manager encouraged me to apply for a **(d)** ________ as a senior support worker – she assured me I had the skills and qualities they'd be looking for. I've been in my new job for over six months now. At my first **(e)** _____________, my **(f)** ___________ suggested I study for my Level 5 Diploma in Management. I'm now training to be a team leader.

5 Describe your career pathway to date. Use the terms introduced in this section.

Applying for a job in social care

1 Choose the correct expression from the boxes to complete these definitions.

application form	~~candidate~~	DBS (Disclosure and Barring Service) check
panel interview	offer	person specification
reference	shortlist	

a Someone who is competing with others to get a job is a *candidate*.

b An ___________ is a document containing questions that a candidate answers to try to get a job.

c A ____________ refers to the section of the application form that outlines the qualifications and professional and personal qualities that a candidate must possess.

d Names of candidates who are most suitable for a job are put on a ____________.

e An _____________ is a formal request asking someone to accept a job.

f A _________________ is used to find out if someone has committed a crime and is, therefore, not suitable for the job.

g A _______________ is where two or more people ask the candidate questions in order to find the best person for the job.

h A ________________ is a statement written about a candidate by someone who can confirm his or her suitability for a post.

2 Number the stages of the hiring process for social carers in the correct order.

a	DBS (Disclosure and Barring Service) checks are carried out and references are checked.	
b	Shortlisted candidates are invited to attend a panel interview.	
c	A contract is signed by the successful candidate and he or she begins work.	
d	A vacancy is advertised and candidates apply by completing an application form.	*1*
e	The successful candidate is informed by telephone and a job offer is then confirmed by letter.	
f	Candidates are shortlisted based on the information in the person specification.	

3 Read about Philip Aketunde and the vacancy he has applied for. What transferable skills do you think Philip possesses?

eg *ability to communicate on the telephone.*

Philip moved to the UK from Nigeria in 2001 with his wife, two sons and elderly father. After 15 years in customer service for a large electrical goods chain, he wants a career change. He has applied to be a care assistant working with the elderly in a residential care home.

SunnyView
CARE

Care assistant

Experience

- Experience gained in a healthcare setting
- Experience with care of the elderly

Skills

- Knowledge of dementia
- Ability to communicate on the telephone
- Good interpersonal skills
- Ability to carry out instructions accurately
- Ability to maintain confidentiality
- Ability to record basic physical observations accurately
- Ability to prioritise workload
- Excellent verbal and written skills
- Ability to use own initiative

4 Write two or three adjectives to describe how you (might) feel before an interview in English. Why?

eg *nervous*

5 🔊 10.3 **Listen to Part 1 of Philip's interview. Underline the words in *italics* to complete these statements.**

a Philip describes himself as *honest and patient / friendly and patient / patient and adaptable*.

b Philip believes being a man would be *difficult / a disadvantage / an advantage* in the care home.

c Philip also possess good *teamwork / management / organisational* skills.

Answering typical interview questions

1 Match a–d with 1–4 to form typical questions in social care interviews.

a	Can you describe what	1	you know they are safe and healthy? If you felt concerned, what would you do?
b	Can you provide an example of how	2	would you maintain their dignity and show them respect?
c	If you were delivering personal support to someone, how	3	type of people or groups you might work with?
d	When going into someone's home, how would	4	you've contributed to effective team working?

2 Why do you think interviewers ask the questions in 1?

3 How confident do you feel about answering the questions in 1? Put a cross (X) on the continuum.

I don't feel confident about answering these questions. ⟷ I feel very confident about answering these questions.

4 🔊 10.4 **Listen and complete a candidate's answers to the interview questions in 1.**

a As a care worker, I'd be working with service users and a team, including other care workers, ______________________________, maybe also social workers.

b In my last job, I worked together with other colleagues to introduce an improved system for communicating with ____________________ daily record.

c First I'd ____________________. I'd make sure ________________, maybe to have a shower or a bath for example. I would try to help the person to ____________________.

d I think I would ________________ and has plenty of food. Then I'd check if there are any ________________________________ or some kind of change in their behaviour. I'd talk to the person to see if there were any problems and then ______________________.

5 '*Tell me what you know about equal opportunities*' is another typical interview question. Write your answer.

6 🔊 10.3 **Re-order the words below to form Philip's response to the question in 5. Then listen to Part 2 of his interview and check your answers. Compare your answer with Philip's.**

and making sure / as part of society. / giving everyone equal access / and that they are valued / It's about / to services and facilities / everyone has a voice

7 🔊 10.3 **Complete Philip's response to the interviewer's next question with the expressions in the boxes. Then listen to Part 2 and check your answers.**

cultural beliefs	daily life of the home	individual personal care needs
respectful way	privacy and dignity	religious calendar events

Sharon: How would you implement equal opportunities in your work with our service users?

Philip: I would make sure that people's **(a)** ____________________ are met in a **(b)** _________ that values their **(c)** __________________, **(d)** ______________. I would also make sure that cultural and **(e)** ______________ such as Ramadan and Christmas were included in the **(f)** __________________.

8 🔊 10.5 **Take the role of the candidate and practise their answers to the questions in activities 1 and 5.**

Attending supervision

1 Supervision is a meeting with your manager to discuss different aspects of your work. What is your experience of supervision in the UK or your own country?

2 Add vowels (*a, e, i, o, u*) to complete these common supervision topics.

a Commun_cat_on sk_lls

b _nd-of-lif_ support (palliativ_ car_)

c D_ath of a r_sid_nt

d New p_licy inf_rmati_n

e Probl_ms car_rs fac_

f P_rformanc_ r_vi_w

3 Read these supervisors' questions. Match them to the correct topic in 2.

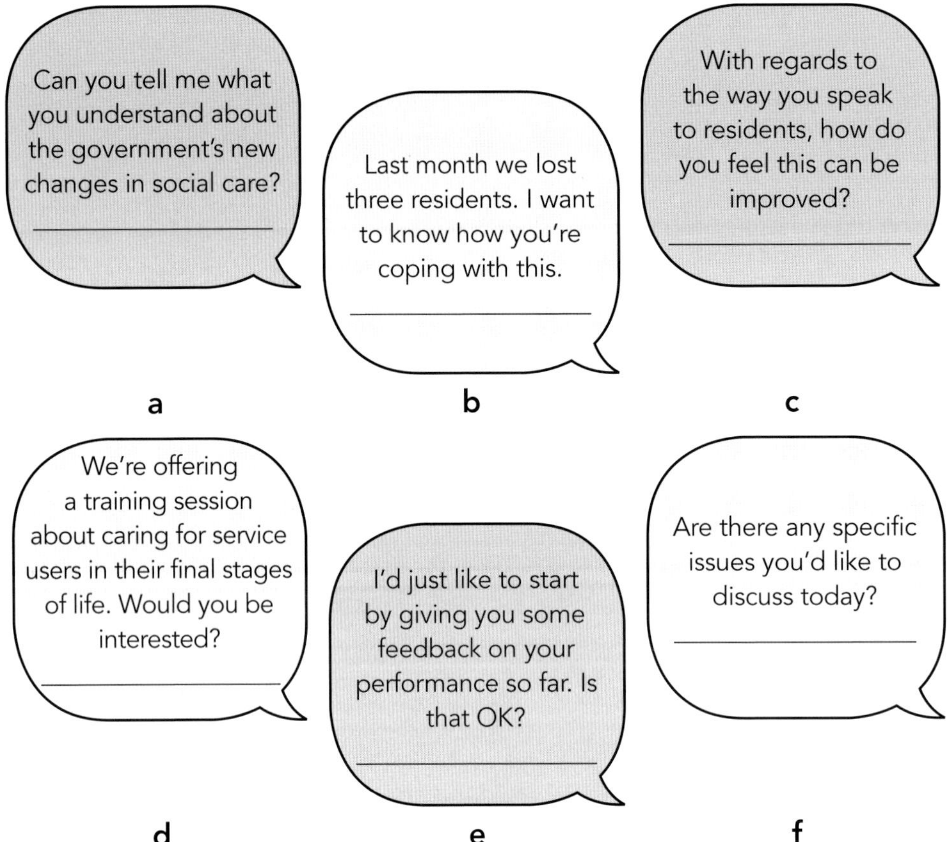

4 10.6 **Listen to Part 1 of Philip's first supervision session. What topics from 2 are they discussing?**

5 10.6 **Listen again. Write *T* (true) or *F* (false) for each statement. Correct any false statements.**

a	Philip wants to talk about studying for Diploma Level 3.	
b	Philip has already completed his Care Certificate.	
c	Philip has demonstrated concern for service users' comfort, privacy and dignity.	
d	Philip is liked by staff and service users for his friendliness.	
e	Philip is a little worried about the feedback so far.	

Receiving feedback

1 Use the words in the boxes to complete the statements about feedback.

colleagues and service users	based on facts	meet the standards
as well as areas for improvement	problem-solving skills	provided in writing
~~false assessment~~	your confidence	

a If you never receive feedback, this can lead to a _false assessment_ of your own abilities.

b Feedback should help you develop skills such as _________ and give you the ability to _________ required of the social care sector.

c Constructive feedback is an essential part of learning and development. It helps you understand your strengths ___________ and can help you develop ___________.

d Formal feedback should be ______________, while informal feedback can take place in discussion with ______________.

e Constructive feedback should be ____________, not on personal characteristics such as intelligence.

2 How do you feel when you receive positive and negative feedback? Why?

3 10.6 **Listen to Part 2 of Philip's supervision session and answer these questions.**

a What aspect of Philip's written communication is the supervisor concerned about?

b What are the possible consequences of Philip's poor writing skills?

c What does the supervisor suggest?

d What is the supervisor's other concern?

e What positive news does the supervisor give Philip?

4 Match the supervisor's statements (1–4) to the correct headings (a–d).

a The supervisor prepares Philip for feedback

b The supervisor asks Philip for consent

c The supervisor offers Philip clarification

d The supervisor encourages Philip to carry out a self-assessment

1 *How about that?*

2 *Let me explain why we're concerned.*

3 *Unfortunately, I have to point out some areas for development.*

4 *Would that be a fair assessment?*

5 Read transcript 10.6 **online and find one or two more examples for each heading in 4.**

6 Re-order the words to form examples of accepting feedback.

a happy with / you're / I'm pleased / my performance

b for me / this is / I accept that / a problem / sometimes

c comments / thanks / I appreciate / your

d your assessment / with / I agree / in the main

e to put / into practice / your suggestions / I'll try

7 Choose an answer from 6 to respond to the supervisor's feedback in a–d. More than one answer may be possible.

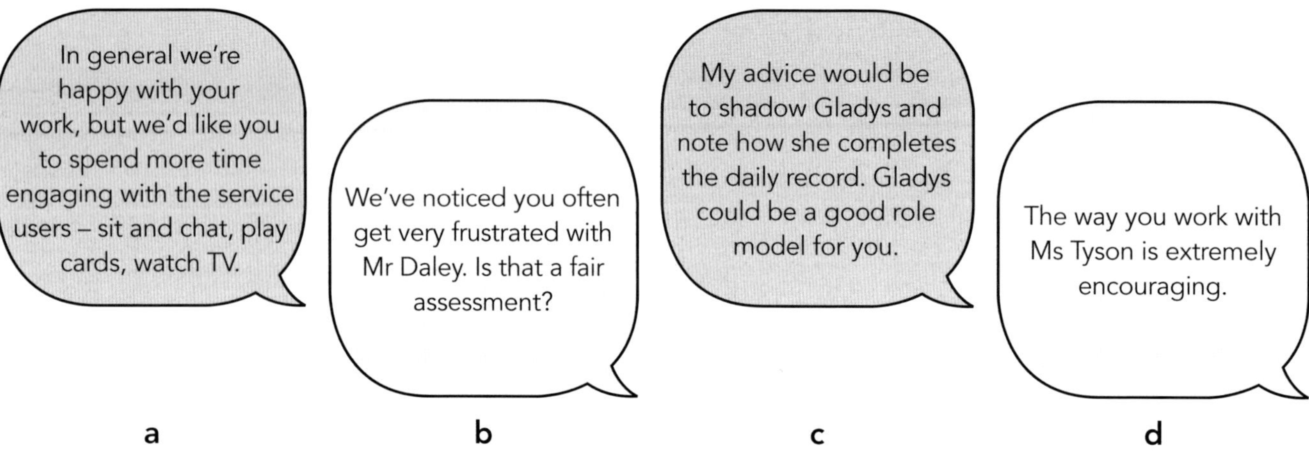

Continued professional development (CPD)

1 Do you think the following are effective ways of developing your professional skills? Why/Why not?

a Taking a training course

b Watching a TV documentary

c Attending a webinar

d Reading a magazine article

e Discussing with colleagues

f Writing a journal article

2 The pictures below show typical topics of training courses. Label them with the titles in the boxes.

Equality awareness	Food and nutrition	Moving and handling
Record keeping	Basic sign language	~~Time management skills~~

a *Time management skills*

b ___________

c ___________

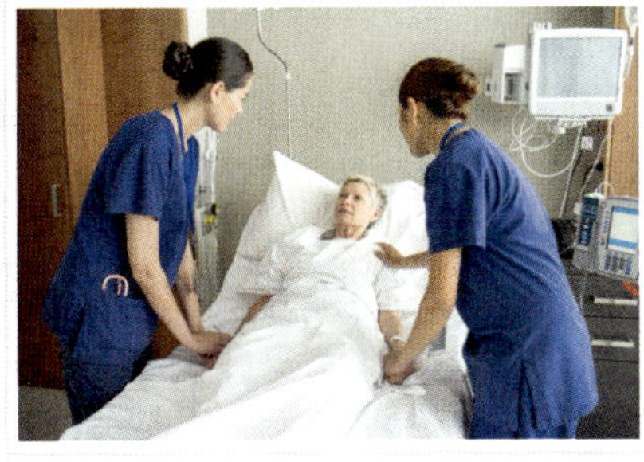
d ___________

e ___________

f ___________

3 Read feedback from these supervisors. Which training course in 2 would be the most appropriate?

1 Maggie finds it difficult to communicate with service users who are hard of hearing.

2 We are concerned about Dale arriving late for appointments.

3 Ravinia struggles to maintain up-to-date records about her service users.

4 Marta isn't aware of policy in the UK for safe movement of adults.

5 As a team leader, it is important that Sanjay demonstrates better cultural understanding.

6 Steve needs to advise service users with learning disabilities on eating a healthy diet.

4 Write two or three more examples of training courses for social carers.

5 Think about your own skills. What training course(s) would you like to attend? Why?

I would be interested in taking a course in … because …

I want to develop my skills in … because …

A language action plan

1 Evaluate the English language skills you have developed during this course. Put an X on the continuum for each unit. Look through each unit quickly and answer the question in the final column.

Unit		I don't feel confident in this area.	I feel very confident in this area.
1	Communication	←———————	———————→
2	Personal care	←———————	———————→
3	Food and nutrition	←———————	———————→
4	Manual handling	←———————	———————→
5	Pain and medication	←———————	———————→
6	Health and safety	←———————	———————→
7	Activities of Daily Living	←———————	———————→
8	Safeguarding	←———————	———————→
9	Challenging situations	←———————	———————→
10	Personal and professional development	←———————	———————→

2 Look through each unit quickly. What exactly do you want to improve? eg asking questions

Unit	
1	______________________
2	______________________
3	______________________
4	______________________
5	______________________
6	______________________
7	______________________
8	______________________
9	______________________
10	______________________

3 As you study, it's also important to improve your general English. You can do this in lots of ways. Answer these questions:

a How do you learn best? (eg *group activities, individually, through reading* etc.)

b When do you learn best? (eg *morning, evening*)

c What do you enjoy doing? (eg *dinner with friends, reading, sport, cinema*, etc)

d How can you do these activities through the medium of English?

4 We met Miro, a carer from Bulgaria, in Unit 1. Read his profile and complete his language action plan. Use the expressions in the boxes below.

Miro arrived in the UK last year with his girlfriend, Albena, and their four-year-old daughter. He trained as a nurse in Bulgaria, but currently works as a carer in the north of England. Miro enjoys playing football, watching films and reading British spy novels. He has a cousin who was brought up in London. He has some free time in the evenings.

emails to my cousin	care issues in English	I have already read	English subtitles
~~also studying English~~	audio books in the car	university students	

Skill	Activity
Speaking	▶ Practise speaking with a colleague who is **(a)** *also studying English*.
	▶ Join a local football team.
	▶ Offer language exchanges with **(b)** ______________ (exchange 30 mins Bulgarian for 30 mins English).
	▶ Chat with cousin via Skype once a week.
Listening	▶ Listen to podcasts about social **(c)** ______________.
	▶ Watch my favourite films with **(d)** ______________.
	▶ Listen to **(e)** ______________ of my favourite spy novels.
Reading	▶ Read online football magazines.
	▶ Read current news items **(f)** ______________ in the Bulgarian press.
Writing	▶ Join my football team's Facebook page to practise sending short messages.
	▶ Write **(g)** ______________ and ask her to correct them / give feedback.

5 Complete your own language action plan below.

Language Action Plan

Skill	Activity
Speaking	
Listening	
Reading	
Writing	